INFORMATION
A sourcebook

Ian Rowlands and Sandra Vogel
with an introduction by Nick Moore

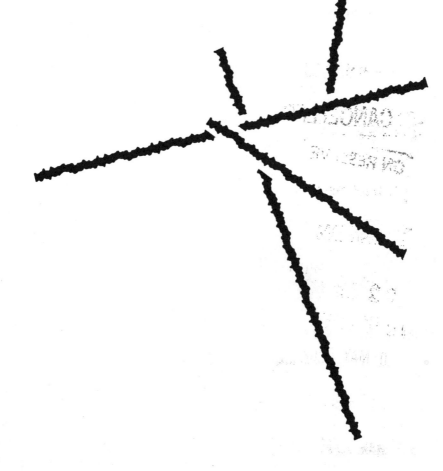

TAYLOR GRAHAM

Published by

Taylor Graham
500 Chesham House
150 Regent St
LONDON W1R 5FA
United Kingdom

Taylor Graham
Suite 187
12021 Wilshire Boulevard
LOS ANGELES
CA 90025
USA

ISBN 0 947568 45 X

CONTENTS

Foreword

This volume is intended as an introduction to a broad and fascinating field of human activity: the creation of policies designed to encourage the realisation of a better information infrastructure. The stakes are high, if we are ever to reach this goal, at least in terms of the likely investment. But then so are the potential rewards: new forms of economic activity; new jobs and career opportunities; and enhanced social provision.

A precondition for success in any field is an awareness and an understanding of its particular problems. Sadly, the literature surrounding information policy issues is often sketchy and incomplete. To make matters worse, there have been relatively few attempts to synthesise existing knowledge, or to develop useful theoretical models. This volume cannot promise to plug such huge gaps in our understanding of information policies and their impact on society. Instead, and working within more modest limits, it is intended as a sourcebook, as a navigational tool for those charting their first paths through the labyrinths of UK information policies.

Perhaps, at first sight, the requirements for such a map are not obvious because — and as anyone will be quick to tell you — the British simply don't have an 'information policy'. In a limited sense, this is true. Certainly, information policies in the United Kingdom are very different from information policies in the United States. The British lack the statutory and constitutional provisions which give clearer form and substance to the contours of Federal information policy — there are, for instance, no direct British equivalents to the First Amendment to the Constitution; or to the Freedom of Information Act. True to the pragmatic character of the British, the landscapes of UK information policy have slowly evolved as a patchwork of smaller, more discrete elements fitting into a more or less harmonious whole. And only the careful observer will be able to perceive its distinguishing features and landmarks.

In this introductory essay, Nick Moore draws boundary lines around the components of modern information policy and shows that, in fact, we need a whole series of maps to fully represent the intricacies of the subject. Sometimes he projects information policies onto regulatory or legislative axes, while at other times they are overlaid onto economic, social and cultural dimensions.

This broad-brush approach brings with it new challenges, because the individual factors which need to be considered when formulating information policies do not, and cannot, stand in isolation — as he points out, information is at the heart of an increasingly complex and sometimes bewildering social system.

The theme of complexity is implicit both in the content of this book and in its rather unconventional format. This reflects a general recognition that it is simply no longer feasible to think in terms of a single, integrated and all-encompassing National Information Policy.

Perhaps a better way to try to understand the overall shape of UK information policies is to look back over time and see how their features evolved. So the next (and longest) section of this book is a densely packed chronology of policy and policy-related events, going back thirty years or so. For the convenience of the armchair orienteer, access to this chronology is offered in the form of 'information policy trails'. These trails should allow the reader to form a quick impression of the key events in, for example, the evolution of personal data protection legislation, or to understand how the British Library has adopted its current organisational structure.

Further study and exploration of information policy issues are encouraged in later sections. These comprise an annotated bibliography of key reports and papers, together with details of relevant contact organisations and suggestions for keeping up-to-date with the ever expanding policy-related literature. Inevitably, there will be gaps and omissions. The authors invite you to help them fill these gaps (and thereby contribute to a planned second edition) by writing to them at the address below.

Finally, a word to our sponsors. Without the support of the National Advisory Body for Public Sector Higher Education (*NAB*), in the form of awards granted under their Selective Research Initiative, the prospects of bringing this work to completion within such a short space of time would have been slight.

IAN ROWLANDS & SANDRA VOGEL
Centre for Communication and Information Studies
Polytechnic of Central London
235 High Holborn
London WC1V 7DN

1. Introduction

There was a time when work on information policy was concerned almost exclusively with the development of a single National Information Policy designed to promote the effective use of scientific and technical information.[5,15,18]* That has now changed. The scope has broadened considerably so that information about science and technology is recognised to be only one element within a more extensive system. Of perhaps greater significance has been the recognition that it is simply no longer practical to think of developing a single all-embracing information policy.[100,103,106]

Information is increasingly seen as a pervasive element in contemporary social and economic life and it raises a wide range of issues which call for some kind of policy response. Despite the importance of information there is, as yet, no strong consensus on what the policy issues are, or how they relate to one another. One way to approach the problem is to consider information policy issues in four broad areas: the issues concerned with legislation and the regulation of information; those concerned with the role of the information sector within the national and international economy; the more local issues which relate to the way information is used within organisations; and the issues concerned with the contribution that information makes to the effective operation of an increasingly complex social system.

LEGISLATIVE AND REGULATORY ISSUES

Information and its use has historically been subject to regulation and control by the state.[24,35] The perceived need for such regulation has grown significantly in recent years as developments in technology have expanded our capacity to produce, communicate, store and retrieve information. It has thus been necessary to redefine and to reinterpret some legislation, such as that relating to copyright, so that it takes full account of new products and other changes brought about by technological advance. In other cases it has been necessary to draft new laws, such as the Data Protection Act, to cope with problems which were not evident before.

---

*The numbers in superscript are pointers to fuller explorations of the issues raised in this introduction. They are intended to direct the reader to relevant material to be found in the third part of this volume: the Annotated Bibliography.

The increased significance attached to information is itself drawing attention to the need for extra controls or legislation. There is, for example, a growing concern that the privacy of individuals is protected.[90],[95] At the same time, there is renewed interest in the concept of freedom of information and in the right to have access to information produced by and about the state.[87],[89] Closely related to this is the recognition that government is a major collector, producer and disseminator of information and that consideration needs to be given to the state's role in the market for tradeable information.[69],[78],[98]

The use of information, and particularly the manipulation of data by machines, is beginning to raise questions of legal liability.[16] While some of these may be resolved through recourse to existing legislation, others may call for new legislation.

In addition there are issues which concern the growing international use and communications of information. Developments such as the rapid uptake of EDI — Electronic Data Interchange — services are raising issues which call for coordinated national responses. Some of these relate to the trading of information services and are currently subject to negotiation in the latest round of GATT discussions,[40] others concern the development of agreements and protocols within international bodies such as the International Standards Organisation.[46]

Most of these issues call for some kind of policy response on the part of national governments or international organisations such as the Commission of the European Communities. There are also matters of regulation which are more properly the concern of the information technology industry. These predominantly concern questions of standardisation.

Many of the issues are complex and have far-reaching implications. Copyright is a case in point. For many years national laws framed within the terms of international conventions served as well. Those few countries which operated outside the conventions were either tolerated or excluded from trading deals. Changes in technology and in the volume of international communication have produced a need to revise both national legislation and international conventions, and this is proving extremely difficult to achieve. Yet the lack of a legislative framework has hampered the development of the information services industry.[50],[56],[65]

MACROECONOMIC ISSUES

Considerable attention has been given to the development of the information sector within the overall economy.[23],[31] Indeed, much of the discussion of the information society is concerned with the growth of the sector of the economy which is responsible for the production of information goods and information services. Yet we have still not developed a reliable method for analysing the sector. We even have difficulties in defining the sector in a consistent and meaningful way.[28,32,34]

There is, however, a general recognition that the information sector is critical to future economic prosperity. If future economic policy is to take account of this there is a pressing need now to measure both the size of the sector and its rate of growth. It is important to do this in such a way that will permit international comparison, for the development of the information sectors in the newly industrialised countries like Singapore, Korea and Taiwan is spawning new competitors in the international marketplace.[13,25]

As well as measuring the developments which are taking place we should consider what government policies might be adopted to foster and assist the expansion of the information sector. This raises major questions about investment in the information infrastructure, particularly in the telecommunications infrastructure.[39,99,103]

There is among economic geographers a growing body of theory which suggests that industrial settlement patterns are being determined by the existence of knowledge centres, in contrast to earlier times when the availability of raw materials or trade routes provided the main impetus to economic developments.[39,41] If these theories are valid, and if we wish to develop our industrial and commercial base, we may need to reassess policies concerning national investment not just in the technical infrastructure but in the human capital of the country.[30,31] This raises significant issues about investment in, and the content of, education and training. We may also need to develop policies which attract and retain highly skilled workers. In the 1960s and 1970s there was a pre-occupation with the brain-drain to the USA. The 1990s could see a similar movement of highly skilled individuals to the Pacific Rim countries.[25]

ORGANISATIONAL ISSUES

Organisations have always used information to control their processes and to make informed decisions. In some cases organisations have developed sophisticated information services to meet particular needs, such as the scientific and technical information services which were developed to support research and development.[107]

In recent years, however, there has been a perceptible shift towards the development of information services which support the management function within organisations. Information is now commonly regarded as a key resource which needs to be managed and developed. Indeed, it is increasingly argued that information and its use can hold the key to gains in productivity within organisations.[23]

To a great extent the situation has developed as a result of the application of information technology. This technology has transformed our capacity to access and manipulate information and it has thus opened up for management the opportunity to use information for decision making on a scale which was not previously possible. Until now managers have had to develop coping mechanisms to enable them to overcome the lack of information. Such coping mechanisms are no longer necessary.

That is not to say that all organisations have changed their way of operating or that managers have found it easy to adjust to an information-intensive way of working. Some organisations have used the technology simply to enable them to do more efficiently what they have always done before. There is growing evidence, however, to indicate that real benefits only arise when organisations radically re-think their style of operation to accommodate the new opportunities which are opening up.

This calls for a recognition that information performs a different function at different levels within an organisation and that the information systems need to be planned accordingly. More particularly there is a need to understand much better the information needs and requirements of managers before installing systems. And this new style of information-intensive management will call for the development of new skills among managers. To be effective they will need to be able to identify and specify their information requirements; to manipulate and handle data and information; to analyse and to synthesise; and to present information in ways which allow it to be easily assimilated.

At a certain level these skills will be required of all managers but the collection and processing of information is a time-consuming task and already there are signs that specialist positions are being created for information analysts to work with groups of managers and policy-makers. This division of managerial labour itself calls for a re-assessment of the management function within organisations.

SOCIAL ISSUES

Just as in organisations, contemporary society is using information more intensively than ever before. At one level there is simply more information available. At another, individuals are being expected to use information more than ever before in order to function more effectively in society.

We are beginning to see a requirement placed upon organisations, particularly those in the public sector, to provide information to enable consumers to make the most effective use of services. The new requirement for schools to publish performance indicators is a good case in point. This raises numerous issues about the reliability and objectivity of information. We are also beginning to realise that we know very little about the extent of unmet need for information or about ways of meeting that need.

Individuals may be given the right to receive information, what is less certain is whether they have the ability to make effective use of it. Recent research suggests that as many as six million members of the workforce lack sufficient levels of literacy or numeracy to enable them to function effectively in society. This raises major questions about the validity of public information systems which depend on printed information. Yet little is known about the effectiveness of alternatives to print.

What has been apparent is the development of a series of networks of advice and information services which are attempting to help individuals and groups cope within an increasingly complex and hostile social structure.

Information technology and the increased use of information within society can hold out the prospect of significant improvements in the quality of life. We must accept, however, that in the short term at least, we are facing the prospect of a growing division between the information rich and the information poor.[24,33]

THE WAY FORWARD

The range of issues which need to be considered is so great that it is obviously not possible to encompass them all within a single National Information Policy. What is called for instead is a process of consciousness-raising. Policy makers and others need to be made aware not only that the issues exist, but that they are related to one another.

The policy responses then need to be formulated on the basis of an understanding of the background to the issues, an appreciation of the need for flexibility in a rapidly-changing environment and an awareness of the inter-connections between the different issues.

NICK MOORE
Policy Studies Institute,
100 Park Village East,
London NW1 3SR

2. Chronology of UK information policy, 1950-1990

INTRODUCTION: INFORMATION POLICY TRAILS

The world of information policy is large and often complex, but one way of making it easier to understand how specific information policies have evolved is to try to think about them in terms of 'hard' and 'soft' factors. Examples of hard factors include events like the setting up of Committees of Inquiry; the commissioning of reports and evaluations by Government; and, of course, the passing of legislation. Soft factors are, almost by definition, less clearly visible within the formal policy framework. Nonetheless, they are equally important in shaping the course of events — they may include milestones in technological research and development; the emergence of an information industry; or the rise of lobbying groups. Both kinds of factors are included in the chronology of policy-related events which follows if they are considered to have made a singificant contribution to the overall development of policies about information in the UK.

This chronological approach brings with it two advantages: it invites the reader to take a necessarily broad view, while at the same time providing a context for specific policy events. The authors hope that this structure will encourage a process of exploration and reflection on the ways in which formal policy has evolved. But, in order to flag attention to a number of important policy strands we suggest a number of 'information policy trails' below. These will allow particular themes to be accessed more easily. The entries in the chronology are numbered sequentially year by year — the trails simply list the entry numbers corresponding to a particular policy theme.

Information Policy Trail 1: Legislation and Regulation

Legislation is the 'hardest' of all the factors impacting national information policy. It is through legislation that Ministerial responsibility for information matters is given and taken away; that advisory bodies are created and given specific remits; and that provision for the information infrastructure is made. Many areas of legislation make some, possibly marginal, reference to information issues. The authors refer readers interested in the full spectrum of legislative matters to the *Encyclopaedia of Information Technology Law* (full details can be found at entry 16 in the Annotated Bibliography). The legislation covered in this section is restricted to that whose central concern is with the development of information policy at national level:

1956; 1959a; 1963a; 1963c; 1964a; 1965a; 1965b; 1965c; 1965d; 1967a; 1968a; 1968b; 1969a; 1970a; 1970b; 1970d; 1971a; 1971b; 1972b; 1973a; 1973b; 1974a; 1975a; 1976a; 1977a; 1978a; 1978b; 1978d; 1978e; 1978g; 1979a; 1979e; 1979f; 1980a; 1980b; 1980e; 1980i; 1981a; 1981b; 1981c; 1981e; 1981f; 1981h; 1982a; 1982b; 1982d; 1982e; 1983b; 1983c; 1983d; 1984a; 1984b; 1984e; 1984f; 1985a; 1986b; 1987a; 1988a; 1988b; 1988c; 1988e; 1989f.

Information Policy Trail 2: **Library and Information Services**

Publicly-funded libraries comprise the backbone of the library and information infrastructure in the UK. Traditionally viewed as separate systems — both in terms of legislation and actual service provision — national, academic and public library services are increasingly seen to be sub-systems of a diverse but integrated network. This trail follows the emergence of new, cooperative approaches to national information provision:

1950a; 1950b; 1957a; 1959a; 1959b; 1964a; 1964b; 1964c; 1967a; 1967b; 1969a; 1970d; 1973a; 1974b; 1975b; 1975c; 1978b; 1978c; 1978d; 1979d; 1979c; 1982c; 1982g; 1982h; 1983f; 1985b; 1986a; 1986c; 1987b; 1987c; 1987d; 1988f; 1990c.

Information Policy Trail 3: **Public/Private Relationships**

Hand-in-hand with the more integrated approach to publicly-funded library and information services in Trail 2, has gone a new emphasis on cooperation between the public and private sectors in service provision. Currently a short trail, this represents a relatively recent shift in policy direction and one which is becoming increasingly important:

1967b; 1982c; 1985b; 1986a; 1987b; 1987c; 1987d.

Information Policy Trail 4: **Electronic Information**

Electronic publishing activities cut across traditional boundaries in service provision and open up new possibilities for information dissemination and access. Advances in information technology have played a major in broadening the scope of the information policy debate — this trail follows some of the key events on the way:

1951; 1957b; 1957c; 1958b; 1959c; 1960a; 1960b; 1962; 1964d; 1965f; 1965g; 1968a; 1968b; 1969b; 1970c; 1970d; 1971b; 1971c; 1971d; 1972d; 1973c; 1976b; 1978d; 1978c;

1978f; 1979b; 1979c; 1979g; 1980d; 1980g; 1981b; 1981g; 1981h; 1981j; 1982a; 1982b; 1983c; 1984c; 1984d; 1984f; 1985d; 1986b; 1986c; 1987a; 1988d; 1988e; 1988f; 1989a; 1989f.

Information Policy Trail 5: Data Protection and Personal Privacy

The growth of personal information held on computers continues to fuel a debate about rights of access and the right to privacy. These concerns are central to the framework of current Data Protection legislation. This Trail traces of the emergence of that legislation:

1970b; 1972a; 1975a; 1976a; 1978a; 1980c; 1981d; 1981e; 1982e; 1984b; 1987f.

1950

1950a
100 YEARS OF THE PUBLIC LIBRARY SERVICE
The centenary of the Public Libraries Act (1850), which firmly established the principle of a free public library service in Britain.

1950b
SCONUL FOUNDED
The Standing Conference on National and University Libraries (SCONUL) is set up to gather data on and coordinate policies between libraries at national and university level.

1950c
NEW SECONDARY PUBLICATION FOR INFORMATION WORKERS
The Library Association begins publication of a new abstracting and indexing tool — Library Science Abstracts.

1951

FIRST COMPUTERISED DATABASES
The world's first computerised (numeric) databases are created at the US Census Bureau, using UNIVAC I, a newly-developed general purpose, commercial computer.

1953

IFLA COUNCIL FORMED
After functioning as a Committee since 1928, the International Federation of Library Associations (IFLA) reforms its internal organisation and adopts a Council constitution.

1956

COPYRIGHT ACT
The provisions of the Copyright Act (1956) clarify and extend UK copyright law, which had remained relatively unchanged since 1911.

1957

1957a

ENHANCED DOCUMENT SUPPLY SERVICES
The National Lending Library for Science and Technology (NLLST) begins operation at Boston Spa in Yorkshire, after a short time in London building and consolidating its stock. Its remit is to act as a central facility for the supply of loans and photocopies of the scientific and technical literature — using as its foundation the many journals taken over from the Science Museum Library.

1957b

EXPERIMENTS IN COMPUTERISED PATENT SEARCHING
The US Patent Office begins experiments with computer patent searching on the National Bureau of Standards SEAC mainframe.

1957c

SPUTNIK LAUNCHED
The Soviet Union launches Sputnik, the world's first artificial satellite.

1958

1958a

NEW PROFESSIONAL BODY FOR INFORMATION SCIENTISTS
A new body — the Institute of Information Scientists (IIS) is set up to promote and maintain high standards in scientific and technical information work and to establish qualifications for those engaged in the profession.

1958b

FIRST COMMUNICATIONS SATELLITES IN ORBIT
SCORE and ECHO I became the world's first operational passive communications satellites to be stationed in orbit.

1959

1959a

ROBERTS' REPORT ON PUBLIC LIBRARIES
The report of the Roberts' Committee on the structure of the public libraries service in England and Wales is published. The Roberts'

Report, which laid the foundations for the 1964 Public Libraries and Museums Act, once more underlined the principle that '. . . the free provision of books has, from the beginning, been the primary object of the public library service and it is, in our view, essential that this principle should be preserved'. [*see Bibliography: entry 121*].

1959b
NEW NATIONAL LIBRARY BUILDING PROPOSED
The Ministry of Works buys land in Bloomsbury (opposite the British Museum) with the cooperation of the London Borough of Holborn. The site is earmarked for the construction of a new building to rehouse some of the national library collections.

1959c
SECOND GENERATION COMPUTERS ARRIVE
IBM develops a range of 'second generation' computers, based on the newly-developed technology of semiconductors. Transistors replace valves for the first time and open up the possibility of much faster and more compact machine processing.

1960

1960a
FIRST PUBLIC DEMONSTRATIONS OF ONLINE SEARCHING
System Development Corporation (SDC) demonstrate an experimental retrieval system for full text called 'Protosynthex'.

1960b
CREATION OF MEDLARS DATABASE
The US National Library of Medicine begins to computerise its information handling procedures, creating a bibliographic file in the process — MEDLARS (Medical Literature Analysis and Retrieval System).

1961

FIRST UK COURSE IN INFORMATION SCIENCE
A new two-year evening course at Northampton College of Advanced Technology, London (later The City University) is set up, leading to the award of the Certificate of the Institute of Information Scientists (the first UK course in information science).

1962

TELSTAR LAUNCHED
The TELSTAR I communications satellite is launched and transmits the first live television pictures between America and Europe.

1963

1963a
INFORMATION FOR SMALL FIRMS
The Department of Scientific and Industrial Research (DSIR) launches an Industrial Liaison Officer scheme to offer technical advice and assistance (often in an information 'gatekeeper' capacity) to small firms.

1963b
NEW UNIVERSITY COURSES IN INFORMATION WORK
A Postgraduate School of Librarianship is set up at the University of Sheffield. The Department of Scientific and Industrial Research (DSIR) approve a new full-time one academic year Diploma course in information science at Northampton College for award of their Advanced Course studentships.

1963c
UNIT FORMED TO PROMOTE INFORMATION RESEARCH
Following the recommendations of the Advisory Council on Scientific Policy (ACSP), the Department for Scientific and Industrial Research sets up a small unit to promote research aimed at finding ways of handling of the rising tide of scientific literature more effectively.

1963d
PUBLICATION OF *LITTLE SCIENCE, BIG SCIENCE*
The publication of *Little Science, Big Science* by Derek J. de Solla Price focuses wide attention on the spectacular growth of the scientific and technical literature — the so-called 'information explosion'.

1964

1964a
PUBLIC LIBRARIES AND MUSEUMS ACT
The Library Advisory Councils for England (LAC-E) and Wales (LAC-W) are set up under the provisions of the Public Libraries and Museums Act (1964) '. . . to advise the Secretary of State (for Education and

Science) upon such matters connected with the provision or use of library facilities whether under this Act or otherwise as they think fit' [*see Bibliography: entry 122*]. The Act is a milestone in the history of the public library service in England and Wales, placing it under the superintendance of the Secretary of State for Education and Science.

1964b

ANNOUNCEMENT OF A NEW NATIONAL LIBRARY BUILDING FOR BLOOMSBURY

Plans were announced for the construction of a new national library building in Bloomsbury. Building is scheduled for the early 1970's at a projected cost to the taxpayer of £10m.

1964c

NEW PROFESSIONAL EXAMINATION FOR LIBRARIANS

The Library Association introduces a postgraduate examination for professional librarians with its own syllabus.

1964d

FIRST ONLINE DATABASE SERVICE

The US National Library of Medicine offers on-demand batch searches of the MEDLARS database for the medical community.

1965

1965a

NEW FRAMEWORK FOR LIS RESEARCH

The Science and Technology Act (1965) provides a broad policy framework within which grants may be allocated to support research and development programmes. Within this new framework, the importance of the emerging disciplines of library and information science is recognised for the first time.

1965b

OFFICE FOR SCIENTIFIC AND TECHNICAL INFORMATION CREATED

An Office for Scientific and Technical Information (OSTI) is set up within the (newly created) Department of Education and Science, following the recommendations of the Advisory Council on Scientific Policy. While OSTI's primary role is to stimulate research and development in the rapidly maturing field of library and information science, its Terms of Reference are fairly wide-ranging:

— to promote research and the development of new techniques and systems;

— to support improvements to existing information services and experiments with new ones;

— to stimulate the education and training of scientists in information work, and in the use of information sources;

— to help coordinate the information activities of Government and the private sector, both nationally and internationally.

Initially, OSTI operates rather like a Research Council, funding research with a strong academic bias as well as more practically oriented studies (including the development of experimental information systems and services — like library automation). From the outset, a financing policy is originated under OSTI which provides seed funding for an emerging electronic database sector, including development grants to the Commonwealth Agricultural Bureaux (CAB); INSPEC; and the United Kingdom Chemical Information Service (UKCIS).

1965c

NEW POLICY MECHANISMS FOR SCI-TECH INFORMATION
Working closely with the newly-created Office for Scientific and Technical Information, a new body, the Advisory Council for Scientific and Technical Information (ACSTI) is set up to play a coordinating role with respect to information policy in science and technology. Drawing its membership from both the government and independent sectors, ACSTI's initial Terms of Reference are:

— generally, to advise the Secretary of State for Education and Science on the conduct of, and support for, UK activities over the whole field of the natural and social sciences and their related technologies;

— more precisely, to advise the Secretary of State on the work of the Office for Scientific and Technical Information (OSTI), and the coordination of this work with that undertaken by other Government departments and independent organisations.

1965d

RE-ORGANISATION OF CIVIL RESEARCH
The report of the Trend Committee in the re-organisation of science in the Civil Service (published in 1963), proposed the formation of a number of new agencies responsible for civil research: [see Bibliography: entry 123]

'. . . the individual agencies will continue, as hitherto, to provide their own information services; but we think that it would be appropriate that the Office of the Minister for Science should assume general responsibility in this field, assisted by a committee drawn from all the agencies concerned.'

15

Thus, the Department for Scientific and Industrial Research is abolished and its previous responsibilities in the areas of scientific and technical information and liaison services to industry are shared between OSTI and the newly-formed Ministry of Technology. Some remaining information responsibilities are distributed between the National Lending Library for Science and Technology and the Research Councils.

1965e
OECD INFORMATION POLICY INITIATIVE
A Scientific and Technical Information Policy Group is set up within the Paris-based Organisation for Economic Co-operation and Development (OECD) in order to foster closer and better links between member nations in the provision of information services.

1965f
NEW STANDARD FOR COMPUTERISED BIBLIOGRAPHIC RECORDS
The MARC (Machine-Readable Cataloguing) programme is initiated at the US Library of Congress to establish an internationally-recognised format for the transfer of bibliographic records.

1965g
FURTHER ADVANCES IN RETRIEVAL SYSTEMS
System Development Corporation develop their ORBIT retrieval software for the US Air Force. Chemical Abstracts Service issue *Chemical and Biological Activities* (CBAC) simultaneously in printed form and on magnetic tape for batch retrieval.

1967

1967a
REVIEW OF UK NATIONAL LIBRARIES
The Secretary of State for Education and Science appoints a Committee under Sir Frederick Dainton to examine 'the various National Libraries, and, in particular, to consider whether these institutions should be brought into a unified framework' [*see Bibliography: entry 124*]

1967b
FOSTERING LIBRARY COOPERATION
A Committee on Libraries is appointed by the University Grants Committee under the chairmanship of Sir Thomas Parry. In his

recommendations, Parry put forward the view that '. . . the entire resources of a geographic area should be regarded as one pool from which each individual library should draw.' [*see Bibliography entry 125*] These are to prove prophetic words in light of subsequent developments in the area of Library and Information Plans (cf **1986a**).

1967c
THE NEED FOR EUROPEAN SCI-TECH INFORMATION POLICY
A basic resolution of the Community Six recognising the need for an overall European scientific and technical research policy is passed. A special group Information and Documentation in Science and Technology (IDST) is set up to look closely at the problem, and to submit proposals for the creation of new information systems.

1968

1968a
OSTI SETS UP DOCUMENTATION PROCESSING CENTRE
As part of OSTI's activities in support of library and information research, a new Documentation Processing Centre is created in Manchester with the following objectives:

— to provide professional support for OSTI's own computer-based projects;

— to provide those engaged in experimental information projects with access to specialised computing facilities;

— to undertake research on computing aspects of the handling of scientific and technical information;

— to contribute to the development and acceptance of standards in computer-based information services.

1968b
FIRST EXPERIMENTS WITH COMPUTERISATION AT HOUSE OF COMMONS
The Office for Scientific and Technical Information sponsors a nine-week project involving the experimental production of a weekly computer-generated current awareness service at the House of Commons Library. Favourably received by MPs, this service provides an encouraging step forward towards the wider use of computers within the Library.

1969

1969a
REPORT OF DAINTON'S NATIONAL LIBRARIES COMMITTEE

The deliberations of Dainton's National Libraries Committee are published. These will later prove to be instrumental in the creation of the British Library (cf 1973a). Despite pressures to set up an authority which would be responsible for the coordination of all library and information activities, the Committee opted instead for '. . . the establishment of a national libraries authority but with functions limited to the operation and development of the existing national libraries'. However, the Dainton Committee was not unaware of the need for better coordination of UK information policy (although this was strictly speaking outside their terms of reference) and made two key recommendations to the Secretary of State underlining: [see Bibliography: entry 124]

> '. . . the desirability of combining all his responsibilities for libraries and for scientific and technical information within a single branch of his department'

> and urging that '. . . Government should examine the feasibility of establishing machinery to provide it with advice on policy concerning the development and co-ordination of national information services.' [see Bibliography: entry 120]

In response to the first of these recommendations, a government-funded national centre for data processing (the Libraries and Information Systems Branch) is created within the DES. Later developments are to see the setting up of ICCSTI, the Interdepartmental Co-ordinating Committee for Scientific and Technical Information (cf 1974a).

1969b
FIRST EUROPEAN ONLINE SERVICE

The European Space Agency (ESA) initiates the first online information retrieval service in Europe, on an experimental basis using NASA's RECON retrieval software.

1970

1970a
DEMISE OF THE LIBRARY AND INFORMATION SYSTEMS BRANCH

The short-lived Library and Information Systems Branch of the Department of Education and Science is closed down and an Arts and Libraries Branch is set up in its place. The new body has a wider brief and absorbs information coordinating responsibilities from different government departments.

1970b

COMMITTEE FORMED TO EXAMINE PERSONAL PRIVACY ISSUES

A House of Commons Committee on Privacy is appointed under Sir Kenneth Younger in May to consider the need growing for data privacy legislation. Its terms of reference embrace the private sector only — both James Callaghan and his successor as Home Secretary, Reginald Maudling, refused to extend the scope of the Committee to include government departments. Instead, it was announced that an internal working party was to be set up to survey the growing use of personal information within government.

1970c

NEW TRADE ASSOCIATION FOR INFORMATION PROVIDERS

Eusidic, a trade association for information providers is founded when four database spinners (two Dutch; one French and one British) decide to get together to exchange experience with software, operations and relations with outside suppliers. Initially, known as the European Scientific Information Dissemination Centres, the name later changes to become the European Association of Information Services by 1990. Eusidic now represents the interests of more than 200 members across both sides of the public/private divide.

1970d

BRITISH NATIONAL BIBLIOGRAPHY COMPUTERISED

The British National Bibliography accepts the US Library of Congress MARC format for the transfer of bibliographic records, but adapts it to local requirements and begin construction of the UK-MARC database.

1971

1971a

DEMISE OF THE INDUSTRIAL LIAISON OFFICER SCHEME

Although still highly regarded in many quarters, the Department of Industry's Industrial Liaison Officer scheme comes to an end with the publication of the recommendations of the Bolton Committee on Small Firms. [see Bibliography: entry 126] However, a number of ILO Centres continue to operate for some time, attached (independently) to selected universities and polytechnics.

1971b

CLOSURE OF OSTI-SPONSORED DOCUMENT PROCESSING CENTRE

The Secretary of State for Education and Science decides to phase out the Department's (specifically OSTI's) work at the Manchester Documentation Processing Centre (DPC). The Centre, established only two years before, is closed in order to reduce Civil Service manpower and to save on departmental costs. However, OSTI continues to promote the functions for which the DPC had been set up, but now by supporting activities in external organisations, such as universities and learned societies.

1971c

FIRST MAJOR US ONLINE DIAL-UP SERVICE LAUNCHED

MEDLINE, the interactive online version of MEDLARS becomes the first operational dial-up information service.

1971d

INTERNATIONAL ONLINE ACCESS DEMONSTRATED

Overseas access to an online database is demonstrated for the first time, between Paris and DIALOG at the Palo Alto Laboratories in California.

1972

1972a

YOUNGER COMMITTEE ON PRIVACY

The Report of the Younger Committee's deliberations on privacy is published in July [see Bibliography: entry 127]. Its main conclusion is that there is no need to establish a general right of privacy under English law. Regarding the use of computers to hold information about individuals, Younger stressed the importance of keeping the possible dangers to privacy in perspective, '... recognising the immense gains to human welfare which computers can bring'. A set of voluntary principles was proposed to regulate the collection and dissemination of personal information in machine readable form and the Committee further recommended that an independent body should be established to review data privacy issues on a continuing basis.

1972b

HUNT INQUIRY ON CABLE BROADCASTING

A Committee of Inquiry is set up to examine issues surrounding cable broadcasting, and the potential of cable systems for delivering new information services (cf 1982d).

1972c

CNAA DEGREES IN LIBRARIANSHIP OFFERED

The first degree courses in librarianship are validated by the Council for National Academic Awards (CNAA), working in close collaboration and agreement with senior examiners appointed by the Library Association.

1972d

MORE PUBLIC ONLINE SERVICES AVAILABLE

The Lockheed Corporation's DIALOG offers the first public online database service, followed shortly afterwards by System Development Corporation's ORBIT service.

1973

1973a

CREATION OF THE BRITISH LIBRARY

The British Library is set up by Act of Parliament [*see Bibliography: entry 128*] as a national centre with three main operational divisions: for reference; lending; and bibliographic information services. The new British Library combines the functions of the British Museum Library; the National Reference Library of Science and Invention (NRLSI); the National Lending Library for Science and Technology (NLLST); the National Central Library (NCL) and the British National Bibliography (BNB).

Interlending services are rationalised with the move of the NCL to Boston Spa in June, extending NLLST's coverage into the humanities and social sciences and thereby constituting a new British Library Lending Division (BLLD).

1973b

WHITFORD COMMITTEE SET UP

A Committee of Inquiry is set up in August under Mr Justice Whitford to consider the existing legislation on copyright and design. Issues under examination include legal deposit, computer software, licensing, and copyright in patents.

1973c

FIRST PUBLIC DEMONSTRATIONS OF VIEWDATA

The first demonstrations of a public videotex system ('Viewdata') is given at the laboratories of the British Telecom Research Centre at Martlesham.

1974

1974a

COORDINATION OF NATIONAL INFORMATION POLICY

ICCSTI, the Interdepartmental Co-ordinating Committee for Scientific & Technical Information is set up by the Department of Education and Science (with a secretariat drawn jointly from the DES and the British Library Research & Development Department in direct response to recommendations of the Dainton Committee. ICCSTI is designed to fulfil two main functions: [*see Bibliography: entry 129*]

> '... one to help harmonise development of policies within individual departments and to look at problems of common concern which are not strictly speaking the sole interest of one department and, secondly, to co-ordinate policy making in relation to the EEC and in the development of a European policy.'

ICCSTI therefore acts as a forum in which the policies adopted by various Government bodies can be reviewed and coordinated. It also acts as a briefing committee for the two UK representatives on the Committee for Information and Documentation in Science and Technology (CIDST), thereby presenting a concerted UK response to information policy initiatives emerging from the Commission of the European Communities (CEC).

1974b

BRITISH LIBRARY RE-ORGANISES ITS BIBLIOGRAPHIC SERVICES

A new British Library Bibliographic Services Division (BSD) is formed around BNB Limited and the Copyright Receipt Office of the British Museum Library. The Bibliographic Services Division exists to satisfy two primary objectives:

— to supply bibliographic services needed by the UK information community (including BLAISE-LINK access to the biomedical and toxicological databases of the US Library of Medicine);

— to support bibliographic records and information processing services (including BLAISE-LINE).

1974c

NEW BODY TO FUND INFORMATION RESEARCH

A new department of the British Library, the Research & Development Department (BLRD&D), is created to fund research activities in the library and information sciences. This new body incorporates OSTI's previously-held responsibilities in the area of science and technology but now expands its remit into other subject areas (in line with the broadened terms of reference of the British Library).

1975

1975a

COMPUTERS AND PRIVACY

In the wake of the Younger Committee's findings, the Government announces its intention to pass legislation to control and regulate possible misuse of personal data stored in machine-readable form. Its White Paper *Computers and Privacy* identified three areas of particular concern:

— inaccurate, incomplete or irrelevant information;

— the possibility of access to information by people who should not or need not have it;

— the use of information in a context or for a purpose other than that for which it was collected.

The Government had clearly reached the conclusion that '. . . the time has come when those who use computers to handle personal information, however responsible they are, can no longer remain the sole judges of whether their own systems adequately safeguard privacy.' [*see Bibliography: entry 130*]

1975b

BRITISH LIBRARY REDEVELOPMENT

In a written reply to Lena Jeger MP (Labour), Hugh Jenkins announces to the House of Commons that work on the first stage of a new British Library building is scheduled to begin in 1980, subject to money being available. This time the site chosen is a 9.5 acre plot in Somers Town, adjacent to St Pancras Station.

1975c

FEWER PUBLIC LIBRARY AUTHORITIES

The implementation of the Local Government Act (1972) leads to a severe reduction in the number of public library authorities in England and Wales.

1975d

CREATION OF THE BNB RESEARCH FUND

A British National Bibliography Fund is set up when the assets of British National Bibliography Ltd are transferred to the British Library. Administered by an independent committee and with a secretariat provided by the British Library Research & Development Department, the Fund exists to support research into the book trade and related literary activities.

1976

1976a
LINDOP COMMITTEE ON DATA PROTECTION
Following publication of the White Paper, Computers and Privacy the previous year, a Committee on Data Protection is established in July under the chairmanship of Sir Norman Lindop. Its task is to advise the Government on the form that any 'permanent control machinery' might take, and to consider the objectives to be incoporated in any future data protection legislation.

1976b
LAUNCH OF DIALTECH SERVICE
Savoy Hill is the location for the first demonstration of the Department of Industry's DIALTECH host service. DIALTECH offers dial-up facilities to the European Space Agency's RECON system based at Frascati (Italy) and provides access to ten (aerospace-oriented) bibliographic files.

1977

1977a
WHITFORD COMMITTEE REPORTS
The deliberations of the Whitford Committee on copyright reform are published. [*see Bibliography: entry 131*]. Among its recommendations are that a number of organisations should be set up, along the lines of the Performing Rights Society, empowered to issue licences to libraries to reproduce certain types of copyright material ('blanket licencing'). Whitford also sought to clarify the legal situation regarding legal deposit, and the copyright status of microforms, patents and computer software.

1977b
100 YEARS OF THE LIBRARY ASSOCIATION
The Centenary Conference of the Library Association is held in London.

1977c
FIRST ONLINE CONFERENCE
The first International Online Conference is held at the Tara Hotel, London in December and attracts more than 400 delegates.

1978

1978a
FINDINGS OF THE LINDOP COMMITTEE ON DATA PROTECTION

The deliberations of the Lindop Committee are published in the form of a substantial document describing the use of computerised records in the UK and how they should be regulated by law. Lindop concluded that a data protection law should be able to '. . . provide a framework for finding a balance between the interests of the individual and those of the data user and community at large.' [see Bibliography: entry 132] At the heart of the proposed legislation would be a Data Protection Authority (DPA), empowered to make rules for data users, to maintain a register of personal data applications and to investigate complaints of misuse. By means of this proposed legislation, Britain would be able to comply with the mounting pressure from international bodies (such as the OECD) to establish the same sort of regulatory controls which were already commonly accepted in other countries.

1978b
NEW COMMITTEE APPOINTED TO REVIEW LIBRARY POLICY

The House of Commons Expenditure Committee, in its eighth report, recommends that the Department of Education and Science should '. . . set up a committee to examine as a matter of urgency, the whole relationship between the department, national, public, university and other libraries, and the Library Advisory Councils' [see Bibliography: entry 133]. The Committee's interest in library matters had been aroused as a result of its scrutiny of selected passages from the Government's White Paper on expenditure planned for the period 1978/9 to 1981/2. In addition to their worries about the apparent lack of coordinatory machinery to deal effectively with the national library system, the Committee also voiced concern over the lack of detailed information on library expenditure.

1978c
GO-AHEAD FOR BRITISH LIBRARY BUILDING

In a statement by the Secretary of State for Education and Science, Shirley Williams confirmed that the (now Labour) Government was giving the final go-ahead for work to start on the first stage of the new British Library building in the Euston Road. Work was due to start 1979/80 at an estimated cost to the taxpayer of £74m.

1978d

GO-AHEAD FOR PARLIAMENTARY ONLINE SYSTEM

In response to the recommendations of the House of Commons Services Committee, a decision is made to proceed with the proposed implementation of a computerised information service of MPs, the Parliamentary Online Information System (POLIS).

1978e

UK ONLINE HOST SERVICE LAUNCHED

Encouraged by ICCSTI, the British Library and the Department of Industry lend support to the creation of a UK national online database host: InfoLine. The new service is launched by a consortium of five partners: the Department of Industry; the British Library; the Chemical Society; the Institution of Electrical Engineers; and Derwent Publications Limited. The scientific databases initially on offer include Derwent's World Patents Index, Chemical Abstracts and Compound Registry, INSPEC and Biosis.

1978f

PUBLIC TELETEXT SERVICES LIMITED

Ceefax (BBC) and Oracle (IBA) broadcast teletext services, which require only a specially-adapted TV set begin full operation in the UK, and are an immediate success with the public.

1978g

MICROPROCESSOR APPLICATIONS PROJECT

The Department of Industry launches an initiative to increase awareness of information technology by offering training, consultancy and project support to commercial firms and public bodies. This initiative is called the Microprocessor Applications Project (MAP) and is funded from a budget worth £55m.

1979

1979a

SUPPORT FOR INNOVATION

The Department of Trade and Industry launches a Support for Innovation scheme to support developments across a wide range of information technology products and services, including: fibre optics; flexible manufacturing systems; robotics; and computer software.

1979b

ONLINE INFORMATION CENTRE FORMED

Aslib's Online Information Centre is set up in March to act as a national information centre for the CEC's new Euronet-DIANE service; and to offer unbiased advice, education and information to UK industry regarding developments in online services. The Centre is jointly funded by the British Library and the Department of Trade and Industry (under its Support for Innovation scheme).

1979c
UK LAUNCHES A PUBLIC VIDEOTEXT SERVICE — PRESTEL
The Post Office launches a public viewdata service, Prestel, and thereby establish a *de facto* standard for British videotex.

1979d
REVIEW OF THE BRITISH LIBRARY SERVICE
In June, an inquiry is set up to examine the information storage and retrieval requirements of the British Library service. Although ostensibly set up to look at the activities of the British Library, the enquiry rapidly developed into much broader investigation of past, present and future methods of information exchange and dissemination, with particular reference to the role of the new information technologies. The work is carried out by the House of Commons Committee on Education, Science and Arts, better known as the 'Price Committee', and the evidence submitted ranges across the whole spectrum of UK information activity: [*see Bibliography: entry 134*]

> '. . . the inquiry has been chiefly concerned to examine the implications of new technologies in the development of libraries in this country. Disquiet has been expressed for some years past about the lack of co-ordination in the library field. We have therefore looked at the role of the new Office of Arts and Libraries . . . as the government department responsible for policy, and at the British Library as the leading institution in the application of new technologies . . . library information services and information services generally are inextricably linked, and an inquiry into overall information policy is overdue.'

The Select Committee made two specific recommendations to Government. One, that a Minister of Cabinet rank should be appointed to take full responsibility for national information policy. Two, that a Standing Commission, representative of the wide range of interests concerned with information provision, be established to examine the problems associated with developing a stronger information infrastructure.

1979e
OFFICE OF ARTS AND LIBRARIES CREATED
An Office of Arts and Libraries (OAL) is set up within the Cabinet Office in September, holding a brief for national and public libraries only (academic libraries still remained under the aegis of the Department of Education and Science). The OAL therefore now superintends the work of the British Library.

1979f
RADICAL REPORT ON TELECOMS LIBERALISATION
In an influential report commissioned by the Department of Trade and Industry, Professor Michael Beesley (of the London Business School) recommends a series of radical proposals for the reform and liberalisation of the current telecommunications supply monopoly (cf **1984e**).

1979g
NEW EUROPEAN HOST SERVICE: EURONET-DIANE
Although not formally launched until the following March, the European Commission's Euronet-DIANE online service begins full operation in November. DIANE (Direct Access Network for Europe) is a joint marketing venture by European host services to offer a wide range of scientific, technical and other databases.

1980

1980a
RAYNER LOOKS AT GOVERNMENT STATISTICAL SERVICES
In January, the Minister for the Civil Service asks Sir Derek Rayner to chair an inquiry (the 'Rayner Scrutiny') to look closely at government statistical services. The review is called against a background of growing concern about the costs of statistical collection and the escalating burden of paperwork for small firms. The scope of the inquiry is to:
[*see Bibliography: entry 135*]

> '. . . look at the structure of statistical effort, and determine whether it delivers what Ministers require, makes the best use of the important skills of professional statisticians, and is subject to effective resource allocation control';
>
> '. . . broaden the concept of statistical work';
> and
> '. . . develop the suggestion that the present structure of the statistical services may be part of past policies, not present ones'.

In December, Rayner submits a series of 30 recommendations to the Prime Minister, based on detailed examinations of individual statistical services. One of his principal recommendations is that '. . .there should be more economic charges for statistics produced . . . except for government departments. Thus, for the first time, a very small part of the sunk cost of the Census is being deliberately offset by direct payments from users'. Rayner also considered the potential for the application of information technology; opportunities for interacting with non-Governmental organisations; and the possibility of new services based on Government-held information being developed with the private sector.

1980b
MINISTER FOR INFORMATION TECHNOLOGY APPOINTED
Following the recommendation of the Price Committee for the appointment of a Cabinet Minister with responsibility for information policy, a Minister for Information Technology (outside Cabinet) is appointed with responsibility for the activities of the Information Technology Division of the Department of Industry.

1980c
NEW OECD GUIDELINES ON PRIVACY
The Organisation for Economic Co-operation and Development (OECD) publishes a set of guidelines covering data privacy and transborder data traffic issues. The background to this publication is a concern to ensure the free flow of information without restricting competition, and a forthcoming Council of Europe Convention on data privacy (cf **1981d**). The Council of the OECD make four recommendations 'to advance the free flow of information between Member countries and to avoid the creation of unjustified obstacles to the development of economic and social relations among Member countries': [*see Bibliography: entry 97*]

'. . . that Member countries take into account in their domestic legislation the principles concerning the protection of privacy and individual liberties';

'. . . that Member countries endeavour to remove or avoid creating, in the name of personal protection, unjustified obstacles to transborder flows of personal data';

'. . . that Member countries co-operate in the implementation of the Guidelines';

'. . . that Member countries agree as soon as possible on specific procedures of consultation and co-operation for the application of these Guidelines'

1980d
MAXWELL TAKES OVER A STRUGGLING INFOLINE OPERATION
Robert Maxwell makes an offer to buy the now-struggling InfoLine operation. The offer is accepted by the other members of the consortium who all withdraw together. Up to this moment in time, InfoLine had already sustained losses of about £2m of (mostly taxpayers') funding.

1980e
ACARD'S *INFORMATION TECHNOLOGY* REPORT
The Advisory Council for Applied Research and Development (ACARD) present their deliberations on the IT industry to the Prime Minister in September. Their report, *Information Technology* [*see Bibliography: entry 136*], is concerned with the new ways of manipulating and presenting information offered by developments in

computing and telecommunications. As well as discussing standards, data protection and other legal constraints, ACARD argues that responsibility for the regulation of communications and broadcasting should be exercised by a single government department.

1980f
EURIPA FORMED
A new trade body, Euripa (the European Information Providers Association), is formed to project and promote the interests of the emerging electronic information industry within (and beyond) Europe.

1980g
EXPERIMENTAL ELECTRONIC JOURNAL
The launch of Birmingham and Loughborough Electronic Network Development (BLEND), an 'electronic journal' project funded by British Library Research & Development Department is announced in September. BLEND is a four-year programme — which is designed to explore and evaluate forms of user communication through an 'electronic journal' and information network, and to assess the cost, efficiency and subjective input of such a system. A joint project between the University of Birmingham and Loughborough University of Technology, BLEND is led by Loughborough's Brian Shackel.

As originally conceived, the BLEND project parallels US work on the 'referred papers journal' — a reference to the Electronic Journal project funded by the National Science Foundation. A group of 40 to 50 users — Loughborough Information Network Community (LINC) — is set up in October to study various types of journal and communication. Trial use of LINC starts in November with the production of a fully electronic journal, *Computer Human Factors*, up to pre-publication draft stage, after which it is electronically archived.

1980h
FIRST TRIPARTITE CONFERENCE
The first 'tripartite' meeting between representatives of Aslib, the Library Association and the Institute of Information Scientists is held in Sheffield in September. *Nationwide provision and use of information* forms the theme of this initial meeting.

1980i
POLIS GOES ONLINE
Scicon Computer Services is granted a six-year contract to provide the computer services which will underpin the creation of an online database service, POLIS, at the House of Commons Library. Parliamentary Questions are the first data elements to be included in the online database.

1981

1981a

GOVERNMENT'S RESPONSE TO THE PRICE COMMITTEE

The Government's official response to the Report of the Price Committee is published. The White Paper agrees that, in principle, libraries and information services should be regarded as a single area of concern. However, it was the view of the Government that: [*see Bibliography: entry 134*]

> '... any national policy on information services must be of a very general and flexible kind, allowing the maximum freedom to individual Departments to maintain and develop services for particular groups of users' needs in the most appropriate way ... It follows that individual Ministers must remain free to take whatever action they consider necessary in their particular fields . . . it would be inappropriate to concentrate executive responsibility in the hands of one Minister'

So, while the appointment of a Minister for Information Policy is rejected, the Government indicates that the Arts Minister would take up any matters on information policy 'not covered elsewhere'. And in response to the call for a Standing Commission to look at the need for a national telematic network, the Government states that it would review the composition and function of the Library Advisory Council for England, which already advised the Minister for the Arts on a wide range of issues in the LIS field. In August it was announced that LAC(E) is to be replaced by a new Library and Information Services Council (LISC) with some expansion of its membership and its functions, thus implicating LISC as the Government's chief advisory agency for national policy on library and information services.

1981b

DTI SUPPORT FOR ELECTRONIC INFORMATION SERVICES

In October, the Department of Trade and Industry creates an Information Technology Division, reporting directly to the new Minister of State for Information Technology. The Division's emphasis is very much on hardware — 'information' is dealt with by other parts of the DTI charged with industry sector needs (activated through the network of publicly-supported research organisations). Some funds are made available for information system development and support, justified on the grounds of advancing a particular area of industry. Around £250,000 a year is allocated for 'database subsidy, promotional activities and other information services' targeted mainly at the not-for-profit sector, including universities, Research Associations and public libraries.

1981c

ITAP COMMITTEE FORMED

In a written Parliamentary answer on 2 July, the Prime Minister announces the creation of an IT Unit in the Cabinet Office and the appointment of an Information Technology Advisory Panel (ITAP) to advise the Government on matters and issues relating to information technology. [*see Bibliography: entry 137*]

> '...in order to ensure that Government policies and actions are securely based on a close appreciation of market needs and opportunities, I am appointing a panel of IT advisers who will be available to advise me and my colleagues on all aspects of IT ...In addition, I have established a small team within the Cabinet Office, made up of both permanent officials and personnel on secondment from the private sector. This unit will be a principal link between the advisers and Departments, will help to promote the use of IT within Government, and will seek to ensure the overall coherence of Government policies towards IT, particularly in so far as they span the responsibilities of more than one Department.'

1981d

EUROPEAN CONVENTION ON PERSONAL DATA

The Council of Europe opens, for signature, a Convention for the protection of individuals with regard to the automatic processing of personal data [*see Bibliography: entry 91*]. The Convention requires each of the Council's 20 member states to establish their own data protection legislation. The Convention prescribes minimum rules for data protection, including the data subject's rights to inspect data and seek protection when data is processed or maintained abroad. Council Resolution (73) 22 urged the governments of Member States '...to take all steps which they consider necessary to give effect to the principles' and '...to inform the Secretary General of the Council of Europe, in due course, of any action taken in this field'.

1981e

UK GOVERNMENT ENDORSES NEED FOR ACTION ON DATA PROTECTION

On 19 March 1981, the Home Secretary announces in the House of Commons that the Government is prepared to sign the recent Council of Europe Convention on data protection, and that it intends introduce its own legislation in this area.

1981f

TELECOMS LIBERALISATION

The Telecommunications Act (1981) paves the way for the liberalisation of the telecoms industry and the separation of British Telecom from the Post Office. British Telecom Enterprises is set up as a direct result of the liberalisation of the telecoms equipment market.

1981g

NATIONAL TELETEXT MONTH

October is designated 'National Teletext Month'. The Government claims to have helped the industry by amending legislation to enable halving minimum HP and rental down-payments required for teletext and viewdata sets; providing three million consumer leaflets explaining the new teletext and viewdata services in simple terms; and producing and distributing a bi-monthly newsletter to assist in communication between and within the various sections of the industry and retail and rental trade.

1981h

INFORMATION TECHNOLOGY STANDARDS

The British Standards Institution reshapes its structure to meet the challenge posed by information technology and creates as Information Technology Standards Council. The Council's remit includes responsibility for developing and coordinating standards in data handling, office machinery, printing and stationery, documentation, and micrographics.

1981i

JCC NATIONAL INFORMATION POLICY SEMINAR

In November, the Joint Consultative Committee (JCC) of Aslib, the Institute of Information Scientists, the Library Association, SCONUL and the Society of Archivists organise a seminar to consider issues of national information policy. The purpose of the seminar is to try to influence government by offering a reasoned and detailed national framework for information resources and provision. Specific topics under review include: new technology and its applications; legal aspects of access to information; resource constraints; education and training; and proposals for consultative machinery.

1981j

IBM PERSONAL COMPUTER

IBM introduces a new range of fast, inexpensive 'Personal Computers'.

1982

1982a

IT '82 PROGRAMME

1982 is designated 'Information Technology Year' in a promotional exercise designed to improve understanding of the new information technologies, and a programme of events is planned to reach the general public as well as leaders in business and public administration. Kenneth

Baker, the newly-appointed Minister for Information Technology, commits £600,000 towards funding the Year, with further cash raised from private industry.

Leading figures from the fields of health; education and the arts; leisure; industry and commerce; medicine; finance; government; and the IT industry spearhead the programme by promoting IT in their own particular spheres. Four road trailers travel around the UK, demonstrating the potential of IT and an 'Inside Information' exhibition is organised at the Science Museum. The culmination of IT'82 is a major Conference on the potential of information technology for transforming the British economy, held at the Barbican Centre in December.

1982b
ALVEY COMMITTEE ESTABLISHED
In March, Kenneth Baker, Minister for Information Technology sets up a Committee under J. Alvey (Senior Director of Technology at British Telecom) to advise on the scope for a major collaborative research programme in information technology.

The Alvey Committee recommends that a five-year programme of research and development into advanced information technologies should be established (within a financial envelope of £350m, more than half coming from government). The main areas for Alvey sponsorship are:

— software engineering;

— human/computer interfaces;

— Very Large Scale Integration (VLSI);

— Computer-Aided Design (CAD);

— communications;

— Intelligent Knowledge-Based Systems (IKBS).

1982c
WORKING TOGETHER WITHIN A NATIONAL FRAMEWORK
Working together within a national framework, the Report of a working party of the Library Advisory Council for England is published in March. Its role was to: [*see Bibliography: entry 138*]

'...consider the objectives of libraries and information services of all kinds, and the scope for enhancing and supporting the library and information network and for making better use of available resources. This scope was to include the application of new technology, and improved forms of co-operation at local, regional and national levels'

Working together proves to be a forward-looking report which somewhat broadened the scope of the national information policy debate:

'. . . it is now essential to consider the development of libraries in the context of information services generally. The present report therefore discusses the future development of information services of all kinds, including libraries, recognising that libraries are only one of the means by which information is disseminated'.

By the time this Report was completed and submitted to the Minister for the Arts, LAC(E) had been subsumed within the new Library and Information Service Council (LISC).

1982d
ITAP REPORT ON CABLE SYSTEMS
The Information Technology Advisory Panel publishes its first major Report [*see Bibliography: entry 137*], concerning the potential role of cable systems and the desirability of a major programme of cable installation. ITAP argues that cable could carry TV and radio broadcasts as well as providing a vastly improved channel for new information applications: domestic videotex; electronic mail; wideband business communications; and remote meter reading. The Report claims that the capital investment needed to offer modern cable services (based on a fibre-optic network) to half the population would be of the order of £2,500m.

1982e
WHITE PAPER ON DATA PROTECTION
The Government presents its proposals for legislating in the area of data protection in the form of a White Paper published in April [*see Bibliography: entry 139*]. The principles underlying the legislation are based largely on those formulated by the Younger Committee, and closely follow Articles 5, 7 and 8 of the Council of Europe Convention on Personal Data (cf 1981d).

Under the proposed legislation, a Data Protection Authority would take the form of a Registrar appointed by the Crown.

1982f
INFORMATION TECHNOLOGY INFORMATION ANALYSIS CENTRE SET UP
A New Information Technology Analysis Centre is set up by the British Library Research & Development Department (BLRD&D), to evaluate the impact of IT on libraries.

1982g
WORK BEGINS ON NEW BRITISH LIBRARY BUILDING
A contract for £5m for the construction of the first stage of the new British Library building at St Pancras is placed with Lilley Construction Ltd.

1982h

BRITISH LIBRARY CONSOLIDATES ITS COLLECTIONS

The collections of the India Office Library and HMSO Binderies are deposited in trust with the British Library.

1983

1983a

UNITED NATIONS' WORLD COMMUNICATIONS YEAR

The United Nations designates 1983 as 'World Communications Year' to promote a more balanced development of the world communications infrastructure. The scope of the programme includes postal services, telephones, telex, radio and television broadcasting as well as satellite, terrestrial and marine links.

An example of the imbalance is that three-quarters of the world's 550 million telephones are concentrated in only eight countries.

1983b

MAKING A BUSINESS OF INFORMATION

The Information Technology Advisory Panel's influential Report *Making a business of information* is published in September. Some of the report's recommendations are designed to promote tighter coordination of both Government and private sector efforts: [*see Bibliography: entry 69*].

'. . . we have at present a fragmented UK information industry interacting with a fragmented set of Government responsibilities . . . greater cohesion and purpose in the national effort in this area requires corresponding institutional changes';

'. . . on the private sector side, we see a need for an umbrella representative trade body . . . This body would bring together the various trade and professional bodies now attempting to develop a group consciousness and to make group views known';

'. . . on the government side, the pattern of responsibilities is complex indeed . . . it is quite clear . . . that there is no Department with overall responsibility for considering the development of the tradeable information sector . . . We therefore see three needs: first, for effective Government machinery, whether within one Department or of an inter-Departmental nature, to consider in an integrated manner the issues raised by the growth of information services and the technical developments which underpin them; secondly, for clear Ministerial commitment to the importance of this area and corresponding priority in policies, and thirdly, for one major Department to have responsibility for the co-ordination of policy in the area.'

As well as focusing on what it perceived to be institutional barriers to the further development of the tradeable information sector, the ITAP Committee looked more widely at a range of other issues, and made recommendations calling for:

— liberalisation of the trade in services;

— promotion of technical standards;

— revision of copyright legislation;

— development of advanced software for searching databases;

— provision of better statistics on the tradeable information sector;

— more effort in IT education and training;

— academic studies into the role of information and communication technologies in modern life.

Not the least significant of recommendations urged by ITAP is a recognition that Government itself has a major part to play in the development of the information sector. The public sector is a very large and influential purchaser of information systems and services. Public procurement policies should therefore attempt, wherever possible, to be consonant with supporting the growth of a strong domestic information sector. And by recognising the commercial value of many of its own information resources, Government should stimulate the creation of new products and services by developing closer ties with commercial organisations.

1983c
DTI SUPPORT FOR THE DATABASE SECTOR
Under its Support for Innovation scheme, the DTI's Information for Industry section allocates £5m (out of a total budget of £55m) to help commercial database companies to develop new products and services. The money is to be spent over the next four years in the form of grants, with the intention of funding up to one-third of research and development costs. Over 300 applications are received and the first grants awarded in June.

DTI's IT Division is also involved more directly in the online sector at this time — as the UK agent responsible for the marketing and promotion of the DIALTECH/IRS host service in the UK.

1983d
COPYRIGHT GREEN PAPER
A Green Paper on *Intellectual property rights and innovation* is published. It examines whether current intellectual property rights are well-suited to encouraging innovation in an era of highly sophisticated and complex technology.

1983e
EURIPA GUIDELINES
In December, the European online trade association, Euripa unveils a

series of six guidelines concerning public sector involvement in information publishing activities. The broad thrust of Euripa's argument is that is that governments should provide information services 'only as a last resort' and not distort the free market for information goods and services.

1983f
FURTHER CHANGES AT THE BRITISH LIBRARY
The collections of the National Sound Archive (formerly the British Archive of Recorded Sound) are integrated within the British Library.

1984

1984a
GOVERNMENT RESPONSE TO *MAKING A BUSINESS OF INFORMATION*
The Government broadly welcomed the findings of the ITAP Report *Making a business of information* in July: '. . . the Government agrees with ITAP that there would be an advantage in a more concerted approach to the issues affecting the information sector' [*see Bibliography: entry 75*]. Encouragement is given to the establishment of a trade organisation, but once again, the Government recognises the sovereignty of its various Departments of State in information matters, so there is little prospect of a Ministry for Information being established. Instead, Kenneth Baker, the Minister for Information Technology in the Department of Trade and Industry, is given special responsibility for coordinating activities between Government departments and the private sector concerning the 'tradeable information' sector.

1984b
SAFEGUARDING PERSONAL DATA
The Data Protection Act (1984) passes into law in July, administered by the Home Office, and will be brought progressively into force over the next three years. The Act places new responsibilities on computer users who store personal information. First, to register a formal application with the Data Protection Register; and, secondly, to follow sound and proper practices enshrined in the following 'Data Protection Principles':

1. The information to be contained in personal data shall be obtained and personal data shall be processed fairly and lawfully;

2.   Personal data shall be held only for one or more specified and lawful purposes;

3.   Personal data held for any purpose or purposes shall not be used or disclosed in any manner incompatible with that purpose or those purposes;

4.   Personal data held for any purpose or purposes shall be adequate, relevant and not excessive in relation to the purpose or those purposes;

5.   Personal data shall be accurate and where necessary kept up to date;

6.   Personal data held for any purpose or purposes shall not be kept for longer than is necessary for that purpose or those purposes;

7.   An individual shall be entitled

(a) at reasonable intervals and without undue delay or expense — (i) to be informed by any data user whether he holds personal data of which that individual is the subject; and (ii) to access to any data held by a data user; and (b) where appropriate, to have such data corrected or erased;

8.   Appropriate security measures shall be taken against unauthorised access to, alteration, disclosure or destruction of personal data, and against accidental loss of personal data'. [see Bibliography: entry 140].

The Act is a complex piece of legislation which establishes an independent Data Protection Registrar with a proposed staff of between 20 and 30 non-civil servants. The Registrar may refuse to register a data user if satisfied '. . . that the application is likely to contravene any of the data protection principles above'. Alternatively, a user could be de-registered for non-compliance with the principles. Data subjects have the right to be informed that data about them are being collected, and the right to sue for damages if their data are disclosed without authority. An appeal is possible from a decision of the Registrar to the newly-created Data Protection Tribunal and, ultimately, to the courts.

1984c
DATA BROADCASTING: NEW APPLICATIONS FOR TELETEXT
Under the provisions of the British Cable and Broadcasting Act (1984),

both the BBC and the IBA are given a mandate by the Home Office to operate specialised teletext services for subscribers, using the UHF terrestrial TV networks or satellite communications channels. (This is in addition to their role as suppliers of the existing public paged teletext services Oracle and Ceefax).

These new data broadcasting services are developed and operated by BBC Enterprises Ltd (a wholly-owned subsidiary of the BBC) and by Oracle Teletext Ltd in conjunction with Aircall Teletext Ltd. The BBC's proprietary data broadcasting system BBC Datacast finds a number of commercial applications — for example on the Trading Floor of the London Stock Exchange and in Coral betting shops.

1984d
WIDE AREA NETWORK INFRASTRUCTURE FOR HIGHER EDUCATION
The Joint Academic Network (JANET) is established on 1 April as an X.25 Wide Area network (WAN) providing inter-site access between the DES-funded sites of the UK higher education and research community — replacing ten separate networks which were already in operation. These DES-funded sites are, precisely, the universities and the various institutions of the research Councils. JANET is paid for directly by the Computer Board for Universities and Research Councils (CBURC), and therefore appears to be a 'free' network, since its users are not billed.

At the time of its inception JANET's main function was to provide researchers and academics in the 'hard sciences' with access to supercomputing facilities available at only a few key university centres. In recent years, however, the nature of JANET has changed — information services of several kinds have begun to appear on the network, and its role as a facilitator of communication between members of the academic community has become much more pronounced.

1984e
TELECOMMUNICATIONS ACT
The Telecommunications Act (1984) formally ends British Telecom's monopoly privileges over the provision of public telecommunications services. The Act provides for the licensing of a competitor: Mercury Communications Ltd (a wholly-owned subsidiary of Cable & Wireless). British Telecom takes advantage of its newly acquired commercial freedom to diversify into new information areas: the database sector; teletext; cable TV; satellite; entertainment; and message handling services. Most of these ventures are managed by the Value Added Systems and Services (VASS) division of British Telecom Enterprises.

1984f

CONFEDERATION OF INFORMATION COMMUNICATION INDUSTRIES

A Confederation of Information Communication Industries (CICI) is formed to represent the numerous trade associations and professional bodies which collectively make up the 'information industries'. The establishment of CICI flows directly from the recommendations of the ITAP Report and its initial membership includes: Aslib; the Library Association; the Institute of Information Scientists; the British Library; the publishing industry associations; broadcasters; the music and recording industries; computing services; software publishers and others.

1985

1985a

CHORLEY COMMITTEE ON GEOGRAPHIC INFORMATION SYSTEMS

The Rt Hon Patrick Jenkin appoints a Committee of Enquiry to review developments in the rapidly emerging field of Geographic Information Systems. The Committee, chaired by Lord Chorley, is asked '. . . to advise the Secretary of State for the Environment within two years on the future handling of geographic information in the United Kingdom, taking account of modern developments in information technology and of market need' [see Bibliography: entry 141].

1985b

PUPILS WORKING PARTY SET UP

A working party, PUPLIS, is convened by the Library and Information Services Council and the British Library Research & Development Division to report on the potential scope for developing greater interaction between the public and private sectors in providing library and information services (cf 1987b).

1985c

ECONOMIC & SOCIAL RESEARCH COUNCIL'S PICT PROGRAMME

Responding to a growing recognition of the pervasive and widespread implications of the information and communication technologies (ICTs), the Economic and Social Research Council (ESRC) establishes a major programme of research into the science aspects of the new communication technologies: the Programme on Information and Communication Technologies (PICT).

PICT is conceived as a network of UK researchers based around funded centres, or 'nodes'. The first three nodes are the Centre for Communication and Information Studies (CCIS) at the Polytechnic of Central London; the Centre for Urban and Regional Development Studies (CURDS) at Newcastle University; and the Science Policy Research Unit (SPRU) at the University of Sussex.

1985d

FIRST COMMERCIAL CD-ROM DATABASES

The first commercial CD-ROM drives for personal computers are marketed, shortly followed by the first commercially-available CD-ROM databases (the Library Company's LC MARC and Grolier's Academic American Encyclopedia).

1986

1986a

PARTNERSHIP IN THE LIBRARY SECTOR

The third report of the Library and Information Services Council (LISC) calls for a greater level of partnership and resource sharing among library services. LISC recommends that local authorities should draw up five-year Library and Information Plans (LIPs) for their area: [*see Bibliography: entry 142*].

> '. . . all the library and information services in the area (the public library, academic libraries and other library and information services in the public sector, as well as the industrial, commercial, professional and other library and information services in the private sector) would review what they currently provided and what they wanted to achieve. With this as a base line, they would agree how they could, in their own individual interests, contract with each other to make the best use of the resources in the area. All would negotiate to get what they wanted, to supply what they wished, free or at a charge for the benefit of their users.

Between them, the Office of Arts and Libraries and the British Library Research & Development Department offer grants of up to £40,000 to help selected authorities to produce their own LIPs as case study material. Work on the first three Plans begins the following year at Leicestershire County Council; at Staffordshire County Council; and at the Northern Regional Library System which covers the counties of Cleveland, Durham and Northumberland.

1986b

VANGUARD PROGRAMME LAUNCHED

In October, the Department of Trade and Industry sponsors VANGUARD, another major IT initiative. The objective of VANGUARD is to encourage British industry to take advantage of the opportunities opened up by the new electronic information media.

Three broad types of business-to-business service are included within the broad scope of these new Value Added and Data Services (VADS):

— electronic data interchange (EDI);

— electronic mail;

— online information services.

VANGUARD is a joint initiative between the DTI and the private sector, represented by five leading companies: British Telecom; IBM; INS; Istel; and the Midland Bank. The first phase of the VANGUARD programme is intended to promote general awareness of VADS, through publicity and promotional events, newsletters, and offers of free consultancy. No grants are made available through VANGUARD, although some 'pump-priming' support is released to help new user communities to undertake feasibility studies.

1986c
TOWARDS A NATIONAL ELECTRONIC ARCHIVE
A pilot study — the Knowledge Warehouse Project — is started late in the year to examine the feasibility of creating a national electronic archive. The study, jointly funded by a consortium of British publishers (Publishers Databases Ltd), the Department of Trade and Industry and the British Library looks at the legal, commercial and technical issues associated with setting up a national archive of electronically published works and typesetting tapes as a resource for research and scholarship.

1986d
LEARNING TO LIVE WITH IT
The third and final Report of the Information Technology Advisory Panel is a wide-ranging consideration of the human resource implications, particularly for education and training, of information technology.

1986e
REVISED INFORMATION ADVISORY MECHANISMS
In April, the Prime Minister announces that the work of the Information Technology Advisory Panel is to be subsumed within an existing advisory body, the Advisory Council for Applied Research and Development (ACARD): [*see Bibliography: entry 143*].

'ITAP had fulfilled its purpose of bringing an external viewpoint to Government policy-making during the developing years of information technology. Evolution meant that this advice could be more closely integrated with other sectors of the economy and, to allow this to happen, the Prime Minister decided that ACARD should subsume the responsibilities of ITAP within its broader remit. ACARD has responsibility for reporting on applied research, design and development related to the technology and exploitation of this work, together with that supported through the Department of Education and Science and the Research Councils, in the UK.'

1987

1987a

HANDLING GEOGRAPHIC INFORMATION

Handling Geographic Information, the Report of the Committee of Enquiry chaired by Lord Chorley is published. It considers some of the policy options which are available to the public sector for exploiting its many collections of locationally-referenced information. Chorley stressed that the concept of 'geographic information' covers an enormous range: not only maps and the distribution of natural resources; but also descriptions of infrastructure; patterns of land use; and indications of the health, wealth, employment, housing and voting habits of people. A range of new tools, or Geographic Information Systems (or GIS), have been developed which utilise the ability of computer systems to link these various types of data by means of locational references.

The Chorley Report identified a number of barriers to the use and acceptance of GIS. These included a general lack of awareness of the potential value of GIS, and the related issue of education and training; organisational inertia; and poorly-defined standards. Two specific recommendations of the Chorley Enquiry were concerned with:

— allocating research and development funds to deal with issues specific to Geographic Information Systems;

— coordinating GIS-related activities across a widely dispersed community of users, through the creation of an umbrella body, an Association for Geographic Information (cf **1989f**).

1987b

PUBLIC-PRIVATE CO-OPERATION IN PROVISION OF LIS

Joint enterprise: roles and relationships of the public and private sectors in the provision of library and information services, the deliberations of the PUPLIS Working Party, is published by the Office of Arts and Libraries. The Report presents a state-of-the art review (with case studies) which attempts to shed light on an important area: the interaction between the public and private sectors in the provision of library and information services. The PUPLIS Working Party drew two major recommendations from their observations of public/private interaction at work: [*see Bibliography: entry 83*].

'. . . the first recommendation is for new thinking, new attitudes to be assumed by top managers in the public sector. Without weakening the essential requirements of public accountability, they should be looking for ways of encouraging more imagination, more daring, more experiment within their organisations . . . In their turn, entrepreneurs interested in working with public bodies on new ventures must take some pains to understand the framework within which public business is conducted'

'. . . the second recommendation is for responsible people in both sectors to explore together ways of developing communications, whether through nominated contact points, intermediaries, employment of people who are experienced on the other side of the line, or however, in order to create an environment in which creative ideas — some of which will be worth pursuing — begin to flow.'

1987c
FINANCING PUBLIC LIBRARIES

The Government issues a Green Paper on financing public library services and immediately prompts one of the widest debates on public library provision this century. Its consultative paper raised four topics for discussion and debate: the nature of a free basic service; wider charging; joint ventures; and contracting-out services.

While still committed in principle to a free public library service (in line with ther 1964 Public Libraries and Museums Act), Government was clearly looking for new ways to generate income and improve efficiency. Fundamental to any consideration of charging policy in public libraries is a definition of the minimum, or basic, level of service which may be expected: [see Bibliography: entry 144].

'. . . the Green Paper defines the basic service as, in broad terms, the reference and information services made available free to all individuals, and the lending services of print materials (including special language materials) which they provide without charge to those who live, work or are in full-time education in their area'

Beyond this basic level of service, it was proposed that library authorities should have wider powers to charge in order to attract money for growth. In fact, the Green Paper suggested that public library authorities should set themselves an initial target for gross annual income of £50m (from a present level of £22m). Five specific proposals for implementing a wider charging policy were offered:

— premium subscription services for novels and biographies;

— charging the full economic cost of reserving items;

— limiting 'free' enquiries to those which do not involve the assistance of library staff for long periods of time;

— charging 'non-relevant' individuals for using authorities' 'non-specialist' services;

45

— charging for all non-print materials.

Charging policy is just one component in financing the library service. Two others are considered in the Green Paper: joint ventures (such as sponsorship and publishing) and possibilities for contracting-out services to the private sector.

1987d
INCENTIVE SCHEME FOR PUBLIC LIBRARIES
Richard Luce, Minister for the Arts, announces the setting up of a Public Library Development Incentive Scheme (PLDIS) to encourage new development and increased efficiency in the public library system. Under the provisions of the Scheme, awards may be granted to library authorities to cover 40 per cent of the cost of new initiatives (up to a ceiling of £40,000). Awards under the PLDIS are conditional upon the authority providing the remaining 60 per cent of the funding. Priorities for the initial round of PLDIS awards include:

— projects involving collaboration between public libraries and other libraries or organisations in the private sector which enable new services to be provided, or exiting ones improved;

— feasibility studies into how public libraries can generate more income, contract out elements of public library services, or joint public/private ventures.

1987e
NO PLACE FOR IT MINISTER IN NEW GOVERNMENT
A Conservative Government is returned for a third consecutive term on 11 June. The next day, when Prime Minister Margaret Thatcher announces her new Government, the post of Minister of Information Technology has disappeared.

1987f
DATA PROTECTION LEGISLATION COMPLETE
The data subject access provisions of the Data Protection Act become fully operative.

1987g
MORE PICT CENTRES
In a major expansion of the Economic and Social Research Council's commitment to fund research into the social implications of the adoption of information and communication technologies, three more academic centres join the PICT network (based at the universities of Brunel, Edinburgh and UMIST).

1988

1988a

THE NEXT STEPS

The Next Steps a Report prepared by the Efficiency Unit is published in February recommending a number of radical reforms in the management of the Civil Service. The Report proposed fundamental changes in the way in which the Civil Service operates by calling for:

— a real devolution of power over budgets, manpower, pay, hiring and firing to executive agencies in the areas of activity embracing the 95 per cent of the Civil Service involved in the delivery of services as opposed to advising ministers or policy;

— a change in the British constitution, by law if necessary, to quash the fiction that ministers can be genuinely responsible for everything done by officials in their name [*see Bibliography entry 145*].

Essentially, *The Next Steps* recommended the creation of a number of Civil Service businesses or 'Executive Agencies' (cf 1987g).

1988b

NEW STATUS FOR COMPANIES HOUSE AND HMSO

Companies House and Her Majesty's Stationery Office are nominated to join three other Departments in being granted 'Executive Agency' status, with their own trading budgets and a tighter, more commercial organisational structure.

1988c

UK COPYRIGHT BILL

The Copyright, Designs and Patents Act (1988) is introduced, repealing and replacing existing intellectual property law in the 1956 Copyright and the 1985 Copyright (Computer Software) Amendment Acts.

1988d

EUROPEAN INFORMATION INDUSTRY LOBBIES MERGE

Following the outcome of successful merger negotiations between Euripa (an association mainly representing information providers in the private sector in Europe) and the European Host Operators Group (EHOG), a new trade association for the electronic publishing sector is formed: the European Information Industries Association (EIIA).

Eusidic, the European Association of Information Services, are involved in the merger negotiations from an early point, but eventually decide not to join in the formation of EIIA.

1988e

VANGUARD COMES TO A CLOSE

The Department of Trade and Industry's VANGUARD initiative is officially wound up in December, although some publications continue to be made available throughout the following year.

1988f

ADONIS DOCUMENT SUPPLY TRIALS

The British Library launches its ADONIS document supply service in a worldwide trial. ADONIS, a collaborative venture with four international publishers (Blackwell Scientific, Elsevier, Pergamon, and Springer-Verlag), involves the distribution of more than 200 high use biomedical journals on optical disk (CD-ROM). These disks are distributed among 13 document supply centres (in Europe, North America, Mexico, Japan and Australia) to supply local needs for articles, using workstations developed by the British Library Document Supply Centre (BLDSC) with financial assistance from the Commission of the European Communities.

1988g

EUROPEAN PLAN OF ACTION FOR LIBRARIES

The Commission of the European Communities issue a discussion document describing a proposed five-year Plan of Action concerned with the collaborative development of libraries within the Community. In general terms, the Commission's informal consultations cover the following issues:

— availability and accessibility of modern library services throughout the Community, taking into account existing geographic discrepancies in library and information provision;

— more rapid but orderly penetration of new information technologies into libraries in a more cost-effective way;

— standardisation — practical consequences and economic impact;

— harmonisation and convergence of national policies for libraries.

1988h

IMAGE SEARCHING ON DIALOG

Image searching and retrieval (from the TrademarkScan database) is first offered on a commercial search service, DIALOG.

1989

1989a

GLOBAL INFORMATION ALLIANCE FORMED A group of eleven information industry associations (representing 1,800 information companies) sign an agreement in New York on 9 September to co-ordinate their activities under a new umbrella — the Global Alliance of Information Industry Associations (GAIIA). The US Information Industries Association (IIA) is appointed as the Group's secretariat for the first two years. The other members of the Global Alliance comprise associations from West Germany, Canada, the UK, China, Spain, France, India, Japan, and Jamaica.

1989b

DEVELOPING THE TRADE IN GOVERNMENT-HELD INFORMATION

An agreement is signed on 10 November between HMSO and Information Agents Ltd (a subsidiary of Electronic Publishing Services Ltd). The agreement allows a commercial firm (Information Agents) to act as HMSO's agent in the information marketplace, defining the requirements of information industry companies in terms of government-held information, and working through HMSO, who administer Crown Copyright, to seek to arrange the release of the information concerned.

1989c

CICI LAUNCH POLICY STATEMENTS SERIES

The Board of the Confederation of Information and Communication Industries publishes a series of policy statements in November for discussion. *Towards National Information Policies* is intended to reflect a broad concensus of the views of the CICI membership across twelve commercially important policy areas:

1. Legal Issues — Copyright
2. Legal Rules for Information Transactions
3. Regulation of the Information Industries
4. Telecommunications Infrastructure
5. Global and National Market Development
6. International Trade
7. 1992 The Single European Market
8. Research and Development
9. Government Procurement and Supply
10. Education, Training and Skilled Manpower
11. Standards
12. Miscellaneous: Taxation and Other Pervasive Policies

1989d

SAUNDERS REPORT

In response to a proposal made jointly by Aslib and the Library Association, Professor Wilf Saunders prepares a report [*see Bibliography entry 146*] presenting his own personal view of the need for a unified professional body representing the interests of the whole LIS community. Saunders' report argues the case for a much closer working relationship (ideally merger) between Aslib, the Library Association and the Institute of Information Scientists.

1989e

INFORMATION UK 2000

A programme of linked studies 'to explore likely trends in the way that information will be generated, handled, stored, and used over the next decade and beyond' is established under the funding and direction of the British Library Research & Development Department (BLRD&D) [*see Bibliography: entry 147*].

1989f

ASSOCIATION FOR GEOGRAPHIC INFORMATION

An Association for Geographic Information (AGI) is set up, following the recommendations of the Chorley Report (cf **1987a**). The aim is to coordinate provision of the maps, tables and other machine-readable geographic data required by public utilities and local authorities for planning purposes. The Association's founder members include the Ordnance Survey, IBM and ICL who cooperate in a programme to computerise large quantities of geographic information.

1990

1990a

EUROPEAN INFORMATION MARKET DEVELOPMENT

The Commission of the European Communities prepares its second IMPACT (Information Market Actions) Programme, a five-year plan for developing the European information market over the period 1991-95.

1990b

ACADEMIC COPYRIGHT AGREEMENT

After several years of negotiation, an agreement is reached in January between the Copyright Licensing Agency and representatives of the higher education sector on payment for photocopying. This blanket licensing agreement generates an annual income of about £1m, to be shared between publishers and authors.

1990c
CENTRE FOR THE BOOK
The British Library announces the establishment of a 'Centre for the Book' to promote the significance of the book as a vital part of the cultural, commercial and scientific life of the nation. The aims of the Centre are to cover all areas of production — from the manuscript to the final product. This is to be achieved by promoting exhibitions showing how books are (or have been) printed and bound, and to encourage the discussion of the impact of new technology on the creative process and information exchange.

3. Annotated Bibliography

INFORMATION POLICIES: DEFINITION, SCOPE AND KEY ISSUES

Any progress towards a better understanding of 'information policies' must begin with an attempt, however tentative, to identify the issues and concerns which should properly exercise the minds of policy makers. This first section of the bibliography brings together a number of key contributions which begin to define the scope and extent of legitimate information policy issues.

1.
BENNETT, J. R. *Control of information in the United States: an annotated bibliography.* Westport, CT: Meckler, 1987.

> This bibliography takes as its starting point the process of creating and sustaining a national information policy consensus in the US. Adopting a broad policy definition, the scope of the bibliography covers areas from education to government, and from corporate/military links to the role of the US Intelligence Agencies.

2.
BRAMAN, S. Defining information: an approach for policy makers. *Telecommunications Policy, 13(3)* 1989, 233-242.

> Considers various attempts which have been made to better define 'information', and suggests that the current (US) national information policy debate is being impoverished by the use of a restricted, market-oriented definition.

3.
BUSHKIN, A. A. & YUROW, J.H. Developing national information policies. *Library Journal, 104(16)* 1979, 1752-60.

> Discusses the role and importance of information in society as background to the need for information policies to be clearly articulated at national level. The authors highlight eight aspects which national information policies should address, with particular emphasis being given to the issues of censorship and secrecy.

4.
CHARTRAND, R. L. The politics of information. *Journal of the American Society of Information Scientists, 36(6)* 1985, 376-382.

> An article which examines the political dimensions of information and its role in modern society. Concerned particularly with relations between government as an information provider and the commercial information marketplace.

5.
DUNN, D. A. Developing information policy. *Telecommunications Policy, 6(1)* 1982, 21-38.

Examines the policy implications which flow from the explosive growth in scientific and technical information, particularly information stored in machine-readable form. The author explores a number of issues, ranging from developments in information technology to data privacy, and suggests areas for further research.

6.
FERGUSON, M. (ed.) *New communications technologies and the public interest: comparative perspectives on policy and research.* Newbury Park, CA: Sage Publications (Communications in Society series), 1986.

Considers the role of new information and communications technologies (ICTs) and their impact on public rights of access to information.

7.
GRAY, J. *National information policies: problems and progress.* London: Mansell, 1988.

Examines the question of national information policy from a theoretical perspective. Gray looks at the essential elements of a national information policy; at the means of implementing policy; and at some of the problems that are likely to be encountered. Case studies are used to show how far these approaches may differ, especially between nations in the developed and the developing worlds.

8.
IGHAM, N. Information in national planning — a developing role. *Aslib Proceedings, 36(3)* 1984, 136-143.

Examines the case for a national network of library resources by considering how publicly and privately funded libraries might join forces in providing information services. Describes the events which led to the creation of the Library and Information Services Council (LISC) and the potential role of this body in facilitating such a network. Generally, the author argues in favour of a more positive approach to cooperation on the part of librarians.

9.
INTERNATIONAL FEDERATION FOR INFORMATION AND DOCUMENTATION (FID). *National information policies: a review of the situation in seventeen industrialised countries (compiled by M. W. Hill).* The Hague: FID, 1989.

This comparative survey, carried out by FID on behalf of the UNESCO General Information Programme, reviews information policies and practice in 17 industrialised countries. The survey makes particular reference to the provision of scientific and technical information.

10.
JUDGE, P. Questions of information policy. *Journal of Information*

Science, 14(6) 1988, 317-318.

Comments on the decision of the Australian government to pull back from a firm commitment
to the idea of a national information policy after fifteen years of detailed consideration. Shows
that the government is still involved in information provision on many levels, but questions the
logic of a call for a formalised national information policy.

11.
KARNI, R. A methodological framework for formulating information
policy. *Information and Management, 6(5)* 1983, 269-80.

An attempt to provide a theoretical framework within which to rationalise the formulation of
information policies.

12.
MANN, M. (ed.) *Information policy: a select bibliography* (British
Library Research Paper, 38). London: British Library, 1988 (2nd
edition).

A key bibliography, now in its second edition, concentrating on UK information policy
documents and commentaries.

13.
MOHAMED, D. (ed.) *Formulating a national policy for library and
information services: the Malaysian experience*. London: Mansell, 1988.

Case study material illuminating the special problems and opportunities for developing
information policies in a newly-industrialised country.

14.
MOORE, N. & STEELE, J. *Information-intensive Britain: an analysis of
the policy issues.* London: Policy Studies Institute, 1991.

15.
REYNOLDS, H. Bibliographic guide to issues of national and
international government information policies. *Government
Publications Review, 11(1)* 1984, 1-39.

A guide to the US information policy literature up to and including 1982.

16.
ROSENBERG, V. National information policies. *Annual Review of
Information Science and Technology, 17* 1982, 3-32.

A review article presenting international perspectives on information policy development. A
number of key policy concerns are examined: notably public/private sector interaction;
government-imposed restraints on scientific publishing; questions of privacy and data access;
and information ownership. Consideration is given to the various international arenas where
information policy debates are conducted: these include UNESCO and the OECD. Finally, the
author briefly considers the information policy orientations of the administrations in France,
UK, Australia, Canada and Brazil.

16a

SAXBY, S. (ed.) *Encyclopedia of information technology law*. London: Sweet & Maxwell, 1990 [two loose-leaf volumes].

A reference tool which identifies a basic framework for the emerging field of law which specialises in the legal problems generated by the development and use of modern information technologies. The areas covered include intellectual property, data protection, telecommunications and electronic funds transfer.

17.

UNITED NATIONS EDUCATIONAL, SCIENTIFIC & CULTURAL ORGANISATION (UNESCO) *Information policy objectives*. Paris: UNESCO, 1974.

18.

UNITED NATIONS EDUCATIONAL SCIENTIFIC & CULTURAL ORGANISATION (UNESCO) *Guidelines on national information policies: scope, formulation and implementation*. Paris: UNESCO, 1981.

Two useful publications which offer checklists of the basic elements to be considered in the formulation of national information policy. Both strongly emphasise the role which a solid scientific and technical information infrastructure can play in economic regeneration and national development.

19.

YUROW, J. H. et al. *Issues in information policy*. Washington, DC: US Department of Commerce, 1981.

'Information policy' is recognised as the sum of many essentially disparate parts. This book offers a discussion of some of the key elements in a more comprehensive policy system: these include the dissemination of public information; rights of access; privacy; the regulation of information markets; the creation of information property rights; and information management and training.

INFORMATION, ECONOMICS AND SOCIETY

The interaction between information, information technology and society is a theme which recurs consistently throughout this volume. Indeed, there is a growing recognition that, if properly managed, information can play a significant role in generating new forms of economic activity. The implications for jobs and industrial regeneration are obvious and only serve to highlight the need for informed policy responses.

20.

BATES, B. J. Information systems and society: potential impacts of alternative structures. *Telecommunications Policy 14(2)*, 1990, 151-158.

Argues that the social effects of new information and communication technologies (ICTs) are determined not only by the applications to which they are put, but also by their form and structures and the way in which they are implemented.

21.

BRINBERG, H. R. Information economics: forum for discussion. *Information Management Review, 3(3)* 1988, 65-69.

A consideration of the nature of information in economic terms. Brinberg provides a clear exposition of the problem, and offers a number of definitions of information for purposes of generating a wider debate about information economics.

22.

CULLEN, A. Electronic information services: an emerging market opportunity? *Telecommunications Policy, 14(2)* 1986.

Considers the development of markets for electronic information services (EIS). Two variables, technology and demand, are used to model the past behaviour of the market and to propose a model of information market development for the 1990s. Cullen concludes by outlining policy implications for the 1990s and notes the need for a shift in emphasis towards the stimulation of demand.

23.

LAMBERTON, D. M. The economics of information and organisation. *Annual Review of Information Science & Technology, 19* 1984, 3-30.

A major review of work in the field of the economics of information published between 1974 and 1984. The review includes a section on information policy issues.

24.

LYON, D. *The information society issues and illusions.* Cambridge: Polity Press, 1988.

Examines some of the social and political issues arising from the notion of an 'information society', and attempts to locate information technologies within cultural and political frameworks.

25.

MACKINTOSH, I. *Sunrise Europe: the dynamics of information technology.* Oxford: Blackwell, 1986.

The author argues that, individually, European countries are no longer able to compete successfully with the established might of the United States or the rising power of Japan in the global information and information technology industries. Mackintosh calls for closer collaboration between European nations in all areas of information technology: from the harmonisation of telecommunications standards; to information service provision; and the production of hardware and software.

26.

MARTYN, J. & FLOWERDEW, A. D. J. *The economics of information.* (Library & Information Research Report, 17). London: British Library, 1983.

Report of a British Library-funded meeting of economists, accountants and information specialists held (in the UK) in 1982 to consider the difficult area of the 'economics of information'. This document presents a resume of previous research in the area, together with a summary of the meeting and suggestions for further research in the area.

27.

MILES, I. From the service economy to the information society — and back again? *Information Services & Use, 7* 1987, 13-29.

> The starting point for this paper is a classical economic analysis of the tertiary (or services) sector of production: an approach which is then criticised by the author. Economic theory offers little insight into the nature of service activities in general and information service activities in particular. Other, post-industrial and information society, theories are compared and found wanting. Miles suggests new ways of looking at the tertiary services sector, focusing on technological change and associated policy issues.

28.

MILES, I. (ed.) *Mapping and measuring the information economy* (British Library Research Report, 77). London: British Library, 1990.

> A collection of critical papers which evaluates various approaches to the definition of an information economy, and the role of information and communication technologies in that economy. Existing sources of statistical information in key areas such as the production of ICTs; their diffusion and application; their implications for employment and training; and wider social concerns.

29.

NORA, S. & MINC, A. *The computerisation of society: a report to the President of France.* Cambridge, MA: MIT Press, 1980 [English translation].

> A key report on the future importance of information technologies in French society and the economy. The report stresses the need for government to adopt a more positive role in managing change. The English edition referenced here includes an introduction by Daniel Bell.

30.

ORGANISATION FOR ECONOMIC CO-OPERATION AND DEVELOPMENT (OECD) Committee for Information, Computer and Communications Policy. *Trends in the information economy* (Information, Computer and Communications Policy, 11). Paris: OECD, 1986.

> An assessment of the effect of the new information and communication technologies on employment and the workforce in the countries of the OECD. A number of clear policy implications flow from the findings of this report, which stresses the future importance of agreeing international standards for recording labour force activity in the ICT area.

31.

ORGANISATION FOR ECONOMIC CO-OPERATION AND DEVELOPMENT (OECD) Committee for Information, Computer and Communications Policy. *Information technology and economic prospects* (Information, Computer and Communications Policy, 12). Paris: OECD, 1987.

> The report confirms the growing contribution which IT makes to national economies, and provides evidence of a small rise in service sector employment (at the expense of the manufacturing sector). This shift is seen less as evidence of de-industrialisation, more as the creation of new job opportunities. Government is seen to have a dual role: facilitating the production and uptake of new technologies; while creating optimal regulatory frameworks.

31a
ORGANISATION FOR ECONOMIC CO-OPERATION AND
DEVELOPMENT (OECD) Committee for Information, Computer
and Communications Policy. *Trade in information, computer and
communication services* (Information, Computer and Communications
Policy, 21). Paris: OECD, 1990.

32.
RUBIN, M. R. & HUBER, M. T. *The knowledge industry in the United
States, 1960-1980.* Princeton, NJ: Princeton University Press, 1986.

An attempt to measure the economic size and importance of the 'knowledge industries'
(education; research and development; communications; information services; computers and
telecommunications) in the United States.

33.
TRABER, M. (ed.) *The myth of the information revolution: social and
ethical implications of communication technology.* Newbury Park, CA:
Sage Publications (Communication in Society series), 1986.

A collection of nine papers which examine the notion of the 'information revolution' from an
international perspective. Collectively, these papers highlight the moral and ethical
inequalities that continue to exist between the industrialised nations and the third world, and
challenge the desirability of a 'global information economy'.

34.
WILLIAMS, F. (ed.)*Measuring the information society.* Newbury Park,
CA: Sage Publications, 1988.

A collection of research reports which attempts to study facets of the emerging 'information
society' using Texas as a case in point.

INTERNATIONAL AND SPATIAL DIMENSIONS
OF INFORMATION

*As we enter the last decade of the twentieth century, the information
industries can be identified as one of the largest and most powerful of any
industrial sector. Information is a multi-billion dollar business in which
markets and corporate spheres of influence are increasingly becoming
globalised. The new spatial realities of information offer a policy challenge
on two fronts: first, in terms of regulation – specifically regulating
corporate activity and international data flows; and secondly in harnessing
the opportunities created by information for local and regional
development.*

35.
COLLIER, H. *Information flow across frontiers: the question of
transborder data.* Oxford: Learned Information, 1988.

An introductory essay which emphasises the importance of international data flows in terms of
their economic, political and historical impacts. The author gives consideration to the

characteristics of information transfer through different channels: paper; telecommunications; satellite; and cable. Questions of national sovereignty and cultural integrity are among the issues which frame a discussion of the barriers to free transborder data flows.

36.

CRONIN, B. Transatlantic perspectives on information policy: the search for regulatory realism. *Journal of Information Science, 13(3)* 1987, 129-138.

This paper examines the differing approaches to national information policies adopted within Western Europe and North America, focusing on telecommunications policies and the incompatibility of standards. The implications of the emergence of giant media conglomerates on national policy formulation are considered.

37.

CSP INTERNATIONAL LTD. *International trade in specialised information services.* London: CSP International, 1986.

A detailed analysis of world trade in electronic information services. This study was one of the first to seriously attempt to quantify and monitor flows of electronic information, by means of a detailed industry survey in eleven European countries.

38.

CSP INTERNATIONAL LTD. *The global structure of the electronic information services industry* (British Library Research Paper, 1). London: CSP International, 1986.

An attempt to outline the size and global structure of the electronic information services (EIS) sector. The report sketches profiles of the major players in the information services industry, discusses the economic characteristics of electronic information, and examines the impact of the public and private sectors on EIS market development.

39.

GILLESPIE, A. E. & HEPWORTH, M. E. *Telecommunication and regional development in the information economy: a policy perspective* (PICT Policy Research Paper, 1). London: Economic and Social Research Council/PICT, 1988.

This paper presents a geographical analysis of the UK information economy. It focuses on the telecommunications infrastructure as the prime force eroding regional differences in employment, production and decision-making structures: destroying what the authors call the 'tyranny of geography'. Not all regions or countries are equally well placed to exploit telecommunications fully, and policy intervention is often necessary to ensure the diffusion of infrastructure to less developed areas.

40.

GREY, R. de C. Elements of a general agreement on information trade. *Intermedia, 15(2),* 1987, 18-23.

A critique of national governments for their failure to deliver coherent national information policies — despite the increasing importance of information within the world economy. The author suggests that a General Agreement on Information Trade (GAIT) is needed to parallel GATT, the existing General Agreement on Tariffs and Trade.

41.

HEPWORTH, M.E. *Geography of the information economy.* London: Belhaven Press, 1989.

Hepworth develops a concept of the Information Society as a means of understanding the forces shaping spatial organisation in today's world. The book examines several levels at which the information economy may have a potential influence, including the concept of the 'information city'. The author also examines how technological change, particularly in the field of IT, has radically altered the nature of economic activity and geographical relationships.

42.

KILGOUR, F. G. Public policy and national and international networks. *Information Technology and Libraries, 2(3)* 1982, 239-45.

After a brief comparative discussion of European and US approaches to national information policies, Kilgour discusses the impact of US public policies on the activities of international networks.

43.

LEESON, K. W. Information policy: national strategies, international effects. *Telematics and Informatics, 1(4)* 1984, 395-408.

A synopsis of various national and regional strategies for developing national information policy. Approaches by the UK, Brazil, Japan and the US are contrasted, and elements of the European Commission's ESPRIT programme discussed. Leeson's conclusions focus on the impact of US deregulatory policies on the international policy debate.

44.

ORGANISATION FOR ECONOMIC CO-OPERATION AND DEVELOPMENT (OECD). *Transborder data flows and the protection of privacy.* Proceedings of the Symposium on Transborder Data Flows and the Protection of Privacy, August 20-23 1979, Vienna (Information, Computer and Communications Policy series, 1). Paris: OECD, 1979 [contributions in English and French].

A comprehensive survey of the issues surrounding transborder data flows. Contributions are divided into the following subject groupsing: issues and trends; economic social and legal dimensions; barriers and the principle of free and continuous flow of information.

45.

ORGANISATION FOR ECONOMIC CO-OPERATION AND DEVELOPMENT (OECD) Information, Computers and Communications Policy Division. *Videotex development strategies.* Paris: OECD, 1988.

A report which discusses the comparative development of videotex in eight European countries, Australia, Canada, Japan and the US. Particular emphasis is given to an examination of the role of government policy in each of the countries assessed.

46.

PRESTON, P. *The information economy and the International Standard Industrial Classification (ISIC): proposals for updating the ISIC* (PICT

Policy Research Paper, 6). Oxford: Economic & Social Research Council/PICT, 1989.

Preston argues that the new information and communication technologies have contributed to a major restructuring of the world economy. In turn, this has revealed gaps in the International Standard Industrial Classification (ISIC), a tool used to produce internationally comparable economic indicators. The inability of ISIC to account for the expanding information economy is a serious defect, and the author offers a number of practical suggestions for expanding its coverage.

47.

ROMERO, A. T. *The international regulation of data services: the debate over the trade and development issues.* London: Pinter Publishers, 1990.

The convergence of telecommunications and computer technologies has given rise to an active debate over the regulation and control of data services. This volume presents an overview of the key issues and arguments.

EUROPEAN PERSPECTIVES AND INFORMATION POLICIES

As Britain becomes more fully integrated with the rest of Europe, both economically and socially, there is a pressing need to accommodate the new geopolitical realities of life in the Community – information policies have never existed without reference to wider economic and social dimensions. This section of the bibliography is intended as an introduction to those elements of national and Community-wide policy which are currently in play within the European arena.

48. ABBEL, R. The West German information policy: results of the first and plans for a second governmental programme. *Aslib Proceedings, 38(6/7)* 1985, 193-198.

Outline of the first West German national information programme of 1974 and its background along with discussion of the aims and objectives of the second programme. 1985-1988.

49.

CANISIUS, P. Information policies in Western Europe: some remarks about the present situation. *Aslib Proceedings, 34(1)* 1982, 13-24.

A critical comparative evaluation of information policies in selected European states: the Federal Republic of Germany; Italy; Scandinavia; France; Spain; Belgium; the Netherlands; and Switzerland.

50.

CONFEDERATION OF INFORMATION COMMUNICATION INDUSTRIES (CICI). *The free flow of information: barriers to the development of the information industry in the UK and the EEC* (CICI Policy Statements series). London: CICI, 1986.

A short discussion document outlining the main barriers (mainly technical and socio-cultural) which impede the free flow of information and the growth of electronic publishing both in the UK and within the European Community.

51.
CZERMAK, M. J. New trends in specialised information policy within the Federal Republic of Germany. *Information Services & Use, 6* 1986, 27-33.

Defends the Federal Republic of Germany against criticism that its national information policies tend to work against the development of a united European information market and in favour of its own domestic suppliers.

52.
DBMIST *Le marché français de l'information en ligne: comportements, strategies, tendances.* Paris: La Documentation Française, 1988 [in French].

The results of a questionnaire survey of French online database producers, characterising the size, shape and profitability of the online database sector in France.

53.
DURAND, A. Realité et perspectives de developpement de l'industrie de l'information français. *Documentaliste, 23(2)* 1986, 47-52 [in French].

Summary of the findings of a working party set up in 1985 as part of an inquiry into information systems and services in France. The article analyses the current state of industrial and commercial information supply in France and identifies a serious shortcoming: poor co-ordination between public and private initiatives.

54.
DURIEUX, B. *Online information in Europe.* Calne, UK: European Association of Information Services, 1990.

The published version of a doctoral thesis, this book examines the online information industry in Europe from a number of perspectives. These include a discussion of the nature of information markets; analysis of players in those markets: database producers, vendors/hosts and integrated information providers; and a discussion of public policies in the major European countries towards the development of electronic information services. Durieux also considers demand for online services and examines current and future roles for the professional information intermediary.

55.
DYSON, K. & HUMPHREYS, P. (eds.) *Policy, politics and the new media: the case of Europe.* London: Francis Pinter, 1987.

Illuminates a number of key areas where new technologies are impacting the mass media. Includes articles on media policies in Western Europe; telematics; cable plans; and the printed word.

56.
EUSIDIC. *Interim report on barriers to the development of the European information industry* (Report of the Barriers Group: a joint working party of EUSIDIC and EURIPA). Wilmslow: European Association of Information Services, 1986.

A review of the main barriers to the further development of pan-European markets for electronic information. Identifies both technical barriers, for instance the structure of telecommunications tariffs, and non-technical barriers such as language and the market distortions which may result from public sector involvement in the information market.

57.
HANSEN, I. B. What is required to design a national information policy? Can media policy and information policy be separated? *In:* Ingwersen, P.; Kajberg, L. & Pejtersen, A. M. (eds) *Information Technology and Information Use,* London: Taylor Graham, 1986, 56-63.

This paper discusses the development of a national information policy in Denmark.

58.
HOLMES, P. Prospects for European business information in the free market in 1992. *In: Proceedings of the 12th International Online Information Meeting, 6-8 December 1988, London.* Oxford: Learned Information, 1988, 749-760.

Different requirements exist in the member States of the European Community for disclosing information about companies. The level of detail registered, and the standards for recording that information also vary widely, posing a technical barrier to the development of pan-European business information products.

59.
HOPKINS, M. *Policy formation in the European Communities: a bibliographical guide to Community documentation: 1958-1978.* London: Mansell, 1981.

More than 600 important reports, communications and memoranda prepared by the Commission of the European Communities (*CEC*) during the period from 1958 to 1978 are described in detail. Attention is concentrated on the major blueprints upon which Community policies are based: many of which have a strong information/informatics content.

60.
HOWELLS, J. Market integration, economic location and the development of European information services. *In:* Locksley, G. (ed.) *The Single European Market and the information and communication technologies.* London: Belhaven Press, 1990, 202-213.

This paper looks at the evolution of *CEC* market integration policies in the electronic information sector, and considers how these policies might effect the growth of the European information services market. An extra-European dimension is introduced in the form of US corporate links with European information service providers and distributors, raising the question of who is most likely to benefit from the creation of a Single European Market.

61.
van der LAAN, A. Information policy in the Netherlands. *Aslib Proceedings, 38(6/7)* 1986, 199-204.

Discusses national information policies in the Netherlands and highlights the role of the Nederlandse Irgaan voor de Bevordering van de Informatieverezorqing (*NOBIN*), the Dutch national organisation for information policy.

62.

MARCHAND, M. Telematics in France: panorama and prospects. *Online Review, 12(2)* 1988, 109-117.

French telematics may be considered the world's most highly developed union of telecommunications and computer technology. Marchand traces the development of telematics in France from the first public display of prototypes in 1972 to the situation in 1988, and speculates on the future prospects for expanding telematics services beyond French national boundaries.

63.

MARTYN, J. *Information involvements of the European Community, II* (British Library Research Paper, 19). London: British Library, 1987.

An outline of the main areas in which the Commission of the European Communities is involved in the information sector. Although principally concerned with the activities of Directorate-General XIII, this briefing paper includes information on wider CEC activities; details of CEC publications; and a detailed description of the Green Paper on the establishment of a common market for broadcasting (with emphasis on satellite and cable services).

64.

MARTYN, J. *EEC Information market and library programmes* (Library & Information Briefings, 12). London: Library & Information Technology Centre, 1990.

A brief discussion of the activities of the European Commission, as they relate to the information market. Includes outline descriptions of DG-XIII's IMPACT Programme and of the Plan of Action for Libraries.

65.

ROWLANDS, I. & VOGEL, S. The challenges and opportunities facing the European electronic information industry. *In:* Locksley, G. (ed.) *The Single European Market and the information and communication technologies.* London: Belhaven Press, 1990, 187-201.

A discussion of the development of the electronic information industry in Europe, this article reflects on the role European Community policies may have on its future development. Market development is considered in the light of the many perceived barriers to the development of pan-European information services, and it is argued that the sector is global rather than national in character.

65a

WORLOCK, D. Information policy progress: a UK-EEC update. *Aslib Proceedings, 39(6)* 1987, 193-196.

A brief outline of developments in UK and CEC information policies during 1986. Outlines the Department of Trade & Industry's Tradeable Information and VANGUARD initiatives; examines the roles of European industry associations in developing information policies; and discusses relevant activities within DG-XIII of the Commission of the European Communities.

INFORMATION POLICIES AND THE PUBLIC/ PRIVATE DEBATE

The State has always played a very significant part in the production and control of information and information services. Sometimes, as in the case of media policy, its interventions have been designed to protect national sovereignty or cultural integrity. At the same time, governments are major collectors, producers and disseminators of information in their own right and much policy debate now centres around their role in a more information-aware society. This section deals with emerging markets for tradeable information and looks at the ways in which the public and private sectors can best work together to develop new products and services.

66.
ALLEN, A. J. *The myth of government information* (Viewpoints in LIS, 6). London: Library Association Publishing, 1990.

67.
BERNINGER, D. E. & ADKINSON, B. W. Interaction between the public and private sectors in national information programs. *Annual Review of Information Science and Technology, 13* 1978, 3-36.

A concise, critical review of US Federal-sponsored research into public/private interaction in the provision of information products and services. The review, which covers the period 1957 to 1977 discusses the changing definitions of the 'public sector' over that period, and charts the rise of a third sector, where ownership is not entirely in the hands of either public or private institutions. This third sector, it is argued, plays a vital role in the emergent information sector. Information provision policies do not lend themselves, it is argued, to centralisation or coordination because of the diversity of information seeking groups: clear guidelines are needed to optimise interaction between the public and private sectors.

68.
BURKERT, H. *'Public sector information and the private sector information market', in search for a new legitimacy of information handling.* Koln: Gesellschaft fur Mathematik und Datenverarbeitung, 1990 [in English].

This discussion paper identifies a multitude of regulations which control the flow of information from the public sector to the private sector. The author suggests that private sector interest in public data is involving both sectors in a search for a new rationality to control information handling. A practical case study of Canadian information law and policy is discussed.

69.
CABINET OFFICE Information Technology Advisory Panel. *Making a business of information.* London: HMSO, 1984.

This, the second report of the Information Technology Advisory Panel (*ITAP*), considered public and private sector roles in the UK electronic information sector. Many of the report's recommendations made a significant impact on government thinking, including the stimulation of both public and private sector interest in government-held 'tradeable information' and the establishment of a new umbrella organisation for the information industries: the Confederation of Information and Communication Industries (CICI).

70.
CHARTRAND, R. L. The role of government in the information society. *Journal of Information Science, 5(4)* 1982, 137-42.

Discusses US information policies and programmes in the light of emerging relationships between the public and private sectors. Highlights the increasingly important role which technology plays in the information society, and identifies key elements in US legislation.

71.
COMMISSION OF THE EUROPEAN COMMUNITIES. *Guidelines for improving the synergy between the public and private sectors in the information market.* Luxembourg: Office for Official Publications of the European Communities, 1989.

Member States within the European Community lack the convergent policies necessary to energise the full exploitation of the official data by the private sector and this constitutes a significant barrier to market development. The guidelines offered are an attempt to develop pan-European parity in private sector access to government-held information.

72.
CRONIN, B. & MARTYN, J. *Public/private sector interaction: a review of issues with particular reference to document delivery and electronic publishing* (BNB Research Fund Report, 17). London: Aslib, 1984.

A wide ranging review of the literature on the interaction between the public and private sectors in information service provision, concentrating on the UK and the US.

73.
DAVENPORT, L. & CRONIN, B. Government policies and the information industry — the balance of interests. *Aslib Proceedings, 39(5)* 1987, 159-167.

While the administrations of the Uk, US and France have embraced the notion of a free market for information goods and services, there are structural reasons why such a free market is not yet possible. These reasons include: the entrenched market position of a few very powerful players; the lack of a coherent information policy (which gives power to the larger lobbying corporations); and the promotion of state-supported national information industries in Europe and Japan. The paper's conclusions include a number of tentative solutions to the policy dilemma.

74.
DAVENPORT, L. & CRONIN, B. Value added reselling and public domain data. *Electronic & Optical Publishing Review, 7(1)* 1987, 8-11.

A review of government initiatives in the UK and the US to make public sector data sets available for value-addition and resale by the private sector. The authors identify the kinds of data which are, or might be made, available and draw a distinction between data which are commercially viable and data which are socially important but not marketable.

75.
DEPARTMENT OF TRADE AND INDUSTRY. *Government response to the ITAP Report on 'Making a business of information'.* London: HMSO, 1984.

This formal response to the ITAP Report on *Making a Business of Information* outlines the

Government's proposed policy framework for the electronic information services sector. In particular, it considers government's role as an information supplier and as a stimulator of economic activity in the area.

76.
DEPARTMENT OF TRADE AND INDUSTRY. *Tradeable information.* London: HMSO, 1986.

A series of three pamphlets produced by the Department of Trade and Industry for government bodies and private sector organisations involved in the trade in public data sets. Each of the pamphlets addresses a specific aspect of tradeable information: one introduces the concept of tradeable information; the second is a set of guidelines for government departments in dealing with the private sector; while the third is a set of model contract clauses for the guidance of both public and private sector partners. This documentation has now been updated with the recent publication of *Government-held tradeable information. Guidelines for government departments in dealing with the private sector* (London: Department of Trade and Industry, 1990).

77.
KENT, C. A. The privatising of Government information: economic considerations. *Government Publications Review, 16(2)* 1989, 113-132.

This article delineates the case for and against privatisation, and reviews the various forms privatisation has taken in the US and in other countries. Kent concludes that a strong economic case for government activity in the information services area may be found in the concept of 'merit goods'. Major studies on the privatisation of government information are evaluated by the author.

78.
MARTYN, J. *Public/private sector relationships* (Library & Information Briefings, 5). London: Library & Information Technology Centre, 1989.

A review of the central issues surrounding public/private sector relationships in information service provision. These include: the factors involved in releasing public data for private exploitation; how the public/private sector relationship works in different contexts; (unfair) competition; pricing issues; and questions of market development.

79.
MYERS, J. Priorities and policies — private sector involvement in our fields of interest. *Journal of Information Science, 9(1)* 1984, 1-6.

Delineates two contrasting philosophies of library and information service provision: the economic ('for profit') and the social ('duty'). Presents the public library sector as subject to increasing financial pressures: these make the realisation of the social imperative more and more difficult. Suggests that a way forward is to be found by increasing private sector involvement in the provision of library and information services.

80.
NATIONAL COMMISSION ON LIBRARIES AND INFORM-ATION SCIENCE (NCLIS) Public Sector/Private Sector Taskforce. *Public sector/private sector interaction in providing information services* (Report to the National Commission on Libraries and Information Science). Washington DC: NCLIS, 1982.

A detailed review of individual cases of public/private sector interaction in information service provision in the US. Highlights a number of unresolved conflicts and recommends positive action in respect of these.

81.
NORTON, R. *Charging for library and information services* (Viewpoints in LIS, 1). London: The Library Association, 1988.

Questions of charging for information while still guaranteeing rights of access are complex and often emotively expressed. Norton attempts to define the questions, and considers how, in the light of current socio-economic and user trends, a complete re-appraisal of services might be undertaken.

82.
OAKSHOTT, P. & WHITE, B. *Publishing and information services in the public and private sectors* (British Library Research Paper, 15). London: Plato/Brenda White Associates, 1987.

Report based on a series of case studies of public/private sector cooperative ventures in publishing and information service provision. The empirical evidence is followed by a critical analysis of public/private sector cooperation which identifies a number of key problem areas.

83.
OFFICE OF ARTS AND LIBRARIES. *Joint enterprise: roles and relationships of the public and private sectors in the provision of library and information services* (Library Information Series, 16). London: HMSO, 1987.

This report of the working party on the Roles and Relationships in the Provision of Library and Information Services (PUPLIS) urges that the time is right to consider the potential for relationships between the public and private sectors in the provision of information services. A wide range of issues are discussed: including tendering for services; copyright; staffing; funding (including sponsorship and advertising); and questions of competition.

84.
PARSONS, S. Economic principles in the public and private sectors. *Policy and Politics, 16(1)* 1988, 29-39.

Presents a comparative evaluation of the public and private sectors as entrepreneurs. Suggest that there are fundamental difficulties for the public sector in adopting a more aggressive, commercial stance.

85.
SAVOLAINEN, R. Fee or free? The socio-economic dimensions of the charging dilemma. *Journal of Information Science, 16(3)* 1990, 143-153.

The issue of charging for library and information services involves complicated political and economic problems associated with the balance of public and private interests. Savolainen attempts to show that the charging dilemma can be expressed in terms of the political value of information in society. Existing charging practices are evaluated by focusing on the differences between private and public interests in the production and use of information.

86.

SMITH, E. V. Roles of public and private sector resources in a national information infrastructure. *International Journal of Micrographics & Video Technology, 4(2)* 1985, 91-103.

> Discusses the roles of public and private sectors in Canada, starting from the premise that information is a national resource and cannot be viewed solely as a private sector responsibility. International cooperation is vital in terms of national information infrastructure, and synergy between all parties is stressed as essential for maximum effectiveness.

INFORMATION AND THE INDIVIDUAL

In an era where more and more information about individuals is being captured, stored and retrieved from machine readable files, the need for firm yet sensitive policies to regulate potential misuse is essential. Generally speaking, current policy responses are rooted in two traditions. On the one hand there are strongly held civil liberties arguments concerning data privacy and the rights of individuals to access information about themselves or the activities of their elected representatives. On the other, a call for a more liberal trading regime in personal information is voiced by the private information sector, particularly with respect to the regulation and control of data flows across national frontiers.

87.

BIRKINSHAW, P. *Freedom of Information: the law, the practice and the ideal.* London: Weidenfeld & Nicholson, 1988.

> A review of current law and practice releated to the individual's rights of access to official information.

88.

CHARLTON, S. & GASKILL, S. (eds) *Encyclopedia of data protection.* London: Sweet & Maxwell, 1990 [loose leaf].

> A legal commentary, with full annotations, to the provisions of the UK Data Protection Act (1984).

89.

COOK, J. *The price of freedom.* London: New English Library, 1985.

> A piece of investigative journalism which examines issues surrounding government information and the Official Secrets Act. Cook strongly advances the case for a UK Freedom of Information Act.

90.

COUNCIL OF EUROPE. *New technologies: a challenge to privacy protection?* Strasbourg: Council of Europe, 1989.

> European data protection experts are becoming increasingly concerned about the

impingement of new technologies on personal privacy and the fact that current laws are not sufficient to safeguard these rights. Three key areas of potential concern are identified: telemetry, interactive media and electronic mail.

91.

COUNCIL OF EUROPE *Protection of the privacy of individuals vis-a-vis electronic data banks in the private sector* (Resolution (73) 22 adopted by the Committee of Ministers of the Council of Europe on 26 September 1973). Strasbourg: Council of Europe, 1974.

An important series of guidelines (with explanatory notes) intended to promote personal data privacy. These guidelines seek to guarantee the individual access to information stored about themselves; to ensure that personal data is correct; and to prevent the use of information for purposes other than those for which it was collected.

92.

CROOK, A. Data protection in the United Kingdom: part 1. *Journal of Information Science, 7(1)*, 1983, 15-22; part 2. *Journal of Information Science, 7(2)*, 1983, 47-57.

These two papers present an overview of the issues involved in data privacy and the impact of information technology on the privacy problem. Crook also provides a valuable historical analysis of the policy events which led to the drafting of the UK Data Protection Act (1984).

93.

FLAHERTY, D. H. (ed.) *Privacy and data protection: an international bibliography.* London: Mansell, 1984.

A bibliography relating to how Canada, FRG, France, Sweden, UK and the US have endeavoured to protect personal privacy in the light of the rapid growth of computerised information. The scope of the bibliography includes books, articles and government reports.

94.

HAZELL, R. Freedom of information in Australia, Canada and New Zealand. *Public Administration Review 67(2)* 1989, 189-210.

95.

JONES, M. G. Citizen's right to information: the role of government. *Information Services and Use, 5(1)* 1985, 37-47.

Examines some of the principal policy decisions affecting Congressional information activities. Information as a critical policy resource for effective government and as a tool for efficient institutional management is widely recognised. Jones argues that more should be done at national level to coordinate and promote the dissemination of government information.

96.

NATIONAL COMMISSION ON LIBRARIES AND INFORMATION SCIENCE. *National information policy* (Report to the President of the United States submitted by the staff of the Domestic Council Committee on the Right of Privacy). Washington DC: NCLIS, 1976.

A key US report outlining the need for a national information policy. The approach taken is broadly based and discusses information policy from a number of perspectives — these issues include: Federal information collection; information for commerce; the importance of new technologies; and the internationalisation of information markets.

96a

NORTHMORE, D. *Freedom of information handbook.* London: Bloomsbury, 1990.

96b

ORGANISATION FOR ECONOMIC CO-OPERATION AND DEVELOPMENT (OECD). *Guidelines on the protection of privacy and transborder data flows of personal data.* Paris: OECD, 1981.

Comprehensive guidelines for both OECD member and non-member states on issue relating to data privacy and transborder data flows. The purpose of the guidelines is to facilitate harmonisation between national legislatures in the framing of data protection laws and regulations; to ensure human rights of access; and to promote the free flow of data between nations.

97.

ROBERTS, S. & ROWLANDS, I. *Freedom of information* (Library & Information Briefings, 27). London: Library & Information Technology Centre, 1991.

98.

US CONGRESS Office of Technology Assessment. *Informing the nation: Federal information dissemination in an electronic age* (OTA-CIT-396). Washington, DC: US Government Printing Office, 1988.

A useful report describing the processes of information dissemination, electronic and traditional, used by all US Federal agencies — from Congress to the National Technical Information Service (NTIS) and the national library system. Basically, the report is an assessment of methods for improving dissemination using technology. Attention is also paid to freedom of information and public/private sector issues.

see also
WACKS, R. *Personal information, privacy and the law.* London: Clarendon Press, 1989.

UK INFORMATION POLICIES: COMMENTARY AND ANALYSIS

The penultimate section of this bibliography presents a number of serious attempts, sometimes from very different perspectives, to get behind the mystique and confusion which surrounds UK information policies and practice.

99.

ADAM SMITH INSTITUTE *Communications policy.* London: Adam Smith Institute, 1984.

This so-called 'Omega' report overviews UK government policy regarding cable, new media, broadcasting and postal services.

100.
ANTHONY, L. J. A national information policy for the United Kingdom. *Aslib Proceedings, 33(3)* 1981, 73-82.

A brief historical outline of the development of national policy initiatives in support of information provision in the UK. The starting point is the dissolution of the Department for Scientific and Industrial Research (DSIR) and its replacement by the Office for Scientific and Technical Information (OSTI) in 1965. The author stresses throughout the near impossibility of formulating a single UK national information policy embracing all aspects of information.

101.
ANTHONY, L. J. National information policy. *Aslib Proceedings, 34(6/7)* 1982, 310-316.

Report of a meeting of the Joint Consultative Committee (JCC) comprising *Aslib*, the Institute of Information Scientists (IIS), the Library Association (LA), the Standing Conference on National and University Libraries (SCONUL), and the Society of Archivists. The meeting, held in November 1981, was intended to clarify the directions these bodies wished the government to take in developing a national information policy.

102.
BROWN, R. Towards a national information policy. *Aslib Proceedings, 34(6/7)* 1982, 317-324.

A discussion of the role of government in the formulation of national information policies. Focuses on three major proposals: the establishment of a Cabinet Minister to act as a focal point for information policy; the creation of a national forum for the discussion and formulation of information policy; and the fuller involvement of the wider information community in policy making.

103.
CONFEDERATION OF INFORMATION COMMUNICATION INDUSTRIES. *Towards national information policies: the British information industries.* London: CICI, 1989.

a discussion document outlining policy proposals in 12 areas relating to the information industry proposals are presented in areas which CICI regards as requiring action either from the Commission of the European Communities or the UK Government. Areas covered are: copyright and intellectual property; information products and IT based transactions; the regulation of information industries; telecommunications and the communications infrastructure; global and national market development; international trade; 1992 and the Single European Market; research and development; government procurement and supply of information services; education and training; standards; taxation and other pervasive policies.

104.
GRAY, J. National policies for scientific and technical information: 1. The United Kingdom. *Journal of Information Science, 1(1),* 1979, 43-47.

The key premise of this paper is that while, historically, the UK has been a major publisher of scientific and technical information, information provision in scientific and technical areas must evolve and adapt to meet changing needs. The roles of various institutions involved in national information provision are examined in this light.

105.
GRAY, J. The UK Government's responsibilities for scientific and technical information services. *Aslib Information, 10(6/7)* 1982, 168-170.

Written by John Gray while he was Special Adviser on Information Services at the Office of Arts and Libraries, this paper offers a definitive statement of government responsibilities in the field of scientific and technical information. Discusses policy relating to information provision in the field of STM, and outlines the specific roles of the British Library, the Office of Arts and Libraries, and the Interdepartmental Co-ordinating Committee for Scientific and Technical Information (ICCSTI).

106.
GRAY, J. National information policy — myth or magic? *Alexandria, 1(3)* 1989, 21-30.

Discusses the problematic nature of national information policies — problems ranging from scepticism of their desirability on the part of senior policy makers, to the difficulties presented by the vast range of activities and elements such a policy must cover. Gray then identifies particular areas where a national forum could realistically be applied.

107.
GRAY, J. & PERRY, B. *Scientific information.* Oxford: Oxford University Press, 1975.

Starting from a consideration of the explosive growth of the scientific literature, the authors describe a crisis in information provision. They discuss three ways of tackling the information explosion: harnessing modern technology; developing information centres based on expertise rather than library holdings; and research designed to understand better the ways in which information is communicated and used. The policy implications of these alternatives are discussed.

108.
HARTLEY, J., NOONAN, A. & METCALFE, S. *New electronic information services: an overview of the UK database industry in an international context.* London: Gower, 1987.

An analysis of the UK online database industry and related areas. Includes a discussion of the economics of tradeable information; an examination of database users, suppliers and services; technological infrastructure and developments; and a review of UK, US and European Community national policies for the database sector.

109.
HUMPHREYS, K. W. A national information policy. *Library Association Record, 86(9)* 1984, 362-363.

Approaches the need for a national information policy from a library and information services perspective. Claims that such a policy is essential in the UK and that a national network of information resources of all kinds should be established.

110.
INSTITUTE FOR RESEARCH ON PUBLIC POLICY (IRPP).*Access: information distribution, efficiency and protection. Report of a Conference held at the Glenerin Inn, Ontario, 1987* (the 'Glenerin Declaration'). Ontario: IRPP, 1987.

The report of a meeting of representatives of three organisations from Canada (IRPP), the United States (NCLIS) and the UK (British Library) drawing up a series of recommendations for concerted action by the three governments and calling for a more coherent policy approach to information matters.

111a

JOINT CONSULTATIVE COMMITTEE. *Report of the Working Party on national information policy.* London: Aslib, 1983.

111b

LEWIS, D. A. & MARTYN, J. An appraisal of national information policy in the United Kingdom. *Aslib Proceedings, 38(1)* 1986, 25-34.

Discusses the various elements which comprise the UK information supply infrastructure, and examines information provision in the light of the lack of a coherent national policy. The thrust of the paper is that while the UK lacks a single governmental focus for information policy, a number of bodies (both governmental and non-governmental) are actively involved in the field.

112.

LINE, M. B. National library and information planning. *International Library Review, 15(3)* 1983, 227-243.

Written while he was the Director General of the British Library Lending Division, this personal view outlines the essential functions of a national library and information system and describes the organisations that may be involved in fulfilling those functions. Starting from a print-oriented perspective and concentrating on the structure and organisation of the British Library, the paper pays relatively little attention to information technology.

113.

MALLEY, I. National and international imperatives of a UK national information policy. *Aslib Proceedings, 42(3)* 1990, 89-95.

Argues that progress towards a coherent set of UK information policies is made difficult by the highly fragmented nature of information responsibilities within government: Malley argues that government departments with different information policy responsibilities are unlikely to develop a single co-ordinated policy. However, 1992's Single European Market and the possibilities it opens up for Community-wide policy harmonisation may lever the UK to act sooner rather than later.

114.

MALLEY, I. *National information policy in the UK.* Leicester: IMPC, 1988.

Malley offers a critical historical analysis of national information policies in the UK and outlines the case for a national information policy as a desirable social goal. The report includes detailed consideration of the relevant official documents and other reports and recommendations to Government, and describes any actions subsequently taken.

115.

OFFICE FOR SCIENTIFIC AND TECHNICAL INFORMATION (OSTI). *OSTI - the first five years: the work of the Office for Scientific and Technical Information, 1965-1970.* London: HMSO, 1971.

A valuable insight into the early history of OSTI, and into the rapidly maturing field of research and development in the library and information sciences.

116.

OSBORNE, J. A. A critical examination of progress at government level since 1980 — the UK situation. *Aslib Proceedings, 34(1)* 1982, 1-12.

This paper examines UK information policy achievements to 1981. Discusses the newly realised role of the Department of Trade and Industry and looks at the issues of free versus payed for services.

117.

ROYAL SOCIETY Scientific Information Committee. *A study of the scientific information system in the United Kingdom* (British Library Research & Development Report, 5256). London: Royal Society, 1981.

An influential report into the scientific and technical information infrastructure of the United Kingdom.

118.

STEWART, J. A. The Government's role: creating the right climate for the technological revolution. *Aslib Proceedings, 36*(1), 1984, 1-6.

A view from the government side, stressing the many opportunities created by information technology. Stewart describes government strategy in the promotion of IT in three broad categories: the encouragement of competition; and support for education and for research and development.

119.

THOMPSON, J. K. L. Britain has IT and funds it, too: information wins high priority in the UK. *Bulletin of the American Society of Information Scientists 6(3)* 1982, 12-17.

An explanation of the role of the Advisory Council on Applied Research and Development (ACARD) in directing government policy on the technology side of the information technology equation. Highlights the recommendations of ACARD's 1980 report on information technology and its effects on policy. The article includes details of government research and development funding, with comment on videotex and teletext services.

120.

UNIVERSITY GRANTS COMMITTEE (UGC)/NATIONAL ADVISORY BOARD (NAB) Transbinary Working Group. *Report of the Transbinary Group on librarianship and information studies.* London: British Library, 1986.

The findings of a Working Group established to study the need and resources for library and information studies (LIS) training across the whole of the United Kingdom.

OFFICIAL PUBLICATIONS CITED IN CHRONOLOGY

The (mainly official) publications which follow include some of the most explicit statements of UK information policies. Each is referred to at various points in the Chronology, where an attempt is made to convey something of their flavour as well as placing them in their proper historical context.

121.
ROBERTS COMMITTEE. *Structure of the Public Library Services in England and Wales* (Chairman: Sir S. Roberts). London: HMSO, 1959 (Cmnd. 660). [*see Chronology: entry* **1959a**]

122.
GREAT BRITAIN. *The Public Libraries and Museums Act (1964).* London:HMSO, 1964 (Ch. 75). [*see Chronology: entry* **1964a**]

123.
TREND COMMITTEE. *Committee of Inquiry into the Organisation of Civil Science* (Chairman: Sir Burke Trend). London: HMSO, 1963 (Cmnd. 2171. [*see Chronology: entry* **1965d**]

124.
DAINTON COMMITTEE. *Report of the National Libraries Committee* (Chairman: Sir Frederick Dainton). London: HMSO, 1969 (Cmnd. 4028). [*see Chronology: entry* **1967a** and **1969a**]

125.
PARRY COMMITTEE. *Report of the Committee on Libraries* (Chairman:Thomas Parry). London:HMSO, 1967. [*see Chronology: entry* **1967b**]

126.
BOLTON COMMITTEE. *Report of the Committee of Inquiry on Small Firms* (Chairman: John Everleigh Bolton). London: HMSO, 1972 (Cmnd. 4811). [*see Chronology: entry* **1971a**]

127.
YOUNGER COMMITTEE. *Report of the Committee on Privacy* (Chairman: Kenneth G. Younger). London: HMSO, 1972 (Cmnd. 5012). [*see Chronology: entry* **1972a**]

128.
GREAT BRITAIN. *British Library Act (1972).* London: HMSO, 1972 (Ch. 54). [*see Chronology: entry* **1973a**]

129.
DEPARTMENT OF EDUCATION AND SCIENCE. *Information Storage and Retrieval in the British Library Service, Observations by the Government on the Second and Fourth Reports from the Select Committee on Education, Science and Arts, Session 1970-80.* London: HMSO, 1981 (Cmnd. 8237). [*see Chronology: entry* **1974a**]

130.
HOME OFFICE. *Computers and Privacy,* London: HMSO, 1975 (Cmnd. 6353). [*see Chronology: entry* **1975a**]

131.
WHITFORD COMMITTEE. *Report of the Committee on Copyright and Design Law* (Chairman: John Whitford). London: HMSO, 1977 (Cmnd. 6732). [*see Chronology: entry* **1977a**]

132.
LINDOP COMMITTEE. *Report of the Committee on Data Protection* (Chairman: Sir Norman Lindop). London: HMSO, 1978 (Cmnd. 7341). [*see Chronology: entry* **1978c**]

133.
HOUSE OF COMMONS. *Selected Public Expenditure Programmes: Eighth Report from the Expenditure Committee.* London: HMSO, 1978 (HC 561). [*see Chronology: entry* **1978b**]

134.
PRICE COMMITTEE. *Information Storage and Retrieval in the British Library Service* (Chairman: Christopher Price). London: HMSO, 1980 (HC 767). [*see Chronology: entry* **1979d** and **1981a**]

135.
CABINET OFFICE. *Review of Government statistical services: report to the Prime Minister* (Chairman: Sir Derek Rayner). London: HMSO, 1980. [*see Chronology: entry* **1980a**]

136.
CABINET OFFICE: ADVISORY COUNCIL FOR APPLIED RESEARCH AND DEVELOPMENT. *Information technology.* London: HMSO, 1980. [*see Chronology: entry* **1980e**]

137.
CABINET OFFICE: INFORMATION TECHNOLOGY ADVISORY PANEL. *Report on cable systems.* London: HMSO, 1982. [*see Chronology: entry* **1981c** and **1982d**]

138.
OFFICE OF ARTS AND LIBRARIES. *The future development of libraries and information services. (1) The organisational and policy framework; (2) Working together within a national framework.* (Library and Information Series, 12). London: HMSO, 1982. [*see Chronology: entry* **1982c**]

139.
HOME OFFICE. *Data protection: the Government's proposals for legislation.* London: HMSO, 1982 (Cmnd. 8539). [*see Chronology: entry* **1982e**]

140.
GREAT BRITAIN. *Data Protection Act (1984).* London: HMSO, 1984 (Ch. 35). [*see Chronology: entry* **1984b**]

141.
DEPARTMENT OF THE ENVIRONMENT. *Handling geographic information. Report to the Secretary of State for the Environment of the Committee of Inquiry into the Handling of Geographic Information* (Chairman: Lord Chorley). London: HMSO, 1987. [*see Chronology: entry* **1985a** and **1987a**]

142.
LIBRARY AND INFORMATION SERVICES COUNCIL. *The future development of libraries and information services: progress through planning and partnership.* London: HMSO, 1987. [*see Chronology: entry* **1986a**]

143.
CABINET OFFICE: INFORMATION TECHNOLOGY ADVISORY PANEL. *Learning to live with IT.* London: HMSO, 1986. [*see Chronology: entry* **1986e**]

144.
OFFICE OF ARTS AND LIBRARIES. *Financing our public library service: four subjects for debate – a consultative paper.* London:HMSO, 1988 (CM 324). [*see Chronology: entry* **1987c**]

145.
EFFICIENCY UNIT. *Improving Management in Government: The Next Steps.* London: HMSO, 1988. [*see Chronology: entry* **1988a**]

146.
SAUNDERS, W. L. *Towards a unified professional organisation for library and information science and services: a personal view.* (Viewpoints in LIS, 3). London: Library Association Publishing Limited, 1989. [*see Chronology: entry* **1989d**]

147.
BRITISH LIBRARY. *Information UK 2000.* London: Bowker-Saur, 1991.

4. Author Indexes

Personal Authors

Abbel, R. 48
Adkinson, B. W. 67
Anthony, L. J. 100, 101
Bates, B. J. 20
Bell, D. 29
Bennett, J. R. 1
Berninger, D. E. 67
Birkinshaw, P. 87
Braman, S. 2
Brinberg, H. R. 21
Brown, R. 102
Burkert, H. 68
Bushkin, A. A. 3
Canisius, P. 49
Charlton, S. (ed.) 88
Chartrand, R. L. 4, 70
Collier, H. 35
Cook, J. 89
Cronin, B. 36, 72, 73, 74
Crook, A. 92, 93
Cullen, A. 22
Czermak, M. J. 51
Davenport, L. 73, 74
Dunn, D. A. 5
Durand, A. 53
Durieux, B. 54
Dyson, K. (ed.) 55
Ferguson, M. (ed.) 6
Flaherty, D. H. (ed.) 93
Flowerdew, A. D. J. 26
Gaskill, S. (ed.) 88
Gillespie, A. E. 39
Gray, J. 7, 104, 105, 106, 107
Grey, R. de C. 40

Hansen, I. B. 57
Hartley, J. 108
Hepworth, M. E. 39, 41
Hill, M. W. 9
Holmes, P. 58
Hopkins, M. 59
Howells, J. 60
Huber, M. T. 32
Humphreys, P. (ed.) 55
Humphreys, K. W. 109
Igham, N. 8
Ingwersen, P. (ed.) 57
Jones, M. G. 95
Judge, P. 10
Kajberg, L. (ed.) 57
Karni, R. 11
Kent, C. A. 77
Kilgour, F. G. 42
Laan, A. van der 61
Lamberton, D. M. 23
Leeson, K. W. 43
Lewis, D. A. 111b
Line, M. B. 112
Locksley, G. (ed.) 60, 65
Lyon, D. 24
Mackintosh, I. 25
Malley, I. 113, 114
Mann, M. (ed.) 12
Marchand, M. 62
Martyn, J. 26, 63, 64, 72, 78, 111b
Metcalfe, S. 108
Miles, I. 27
Miles, I. (ed.) 28

Corporate Authors

5. Further reading

NEWSLETTERS

Advanced Information Report
Oxford: Elsevier Science Publishers Ltd.
12 issues a year (ISSN 0953 8712).

News and comment in all areas of electronic publishing and technological developments affecting the storage, dissemination and retrieval of information. Aimed both at information professionals and end-users.

Aslib Information
London: Aslib, The Association for Information Management.
12 issues a year (ISSN 0305 0033).

Contains news of events in the library and information world, details of Aslib activities, book reviews, guest editorials and comment.

EPJournal
London: Electronic Publishing Services (Publications) Ltd.
10 issues a year (ISSN 0954 3244).

An international newsletter focusing on the commercial and business aspects of electronic publishing. Strong on information policy issues as they impact electronic information service activity.

I'M (Information Market)
Luxembourg: Commission of the European Communities (DG XIII-B).
4 issues a year (ISSN 0256 5065).

News about European information products and services, developments in the information market and in European policy relating to the electronic information sector from the Commission of the European Communities.

Inform
London: Institute of Information Scientists (IIS).
10 issues a year (ISSN 0306 0786).

News and information about Institute activities for members, together with coverage of recent developments in the information world.

Information Hotline
New York: Science Associates/International, Inc.
10 issues a year (ISSN 0360 5817).

A newsletter covering developments in US Federal information, telecommunications and related policies.

Information World Review
Oxford: Learned Information (Europe) Ltd.
11 issues a year (ISSN 0950 9879).

The widest circulation newspaper for the electronic publishing industry. Contains new product information, personnel changes, articles on telecommunications and technical innovation, plus coverage of public policy issues.

Infotecture Europe (European edition)
Luxembourg: Transtex International.
22 issues a year (ISSN 0294 7544), also available online (full text) as the IID database.

Contains product information, news and reviews relating to the electronic information services industry. Focuses largely on Europe but sometimes includes material relating to the US, Japan and other countries.

Monitor
Oxford: Learned Information Ltd.
12 issues a year (no ISSN).

An analytical review of current events in electronic information.

Unisist Newsletter
Paris: Unisist, on behalf of the UNESCO General Information Programme.
4 issues a year (ISSN 0379 2218).

This newsletter provides current information on UNESCO's activities in the field of scientific and technical information, documentation, libraries and archives.

JOURNALS

Alexandria
Aldershot: Gower Publishing Co. Ltd, on behalf of the British Library.
3 issues a year (ISSN 0955 7490).

National library and international policy issues of interest to library and information professionals, especially those working in national and major research libraries. Also of interest to those concerned with national policy and information policy planning, or involved in international co-operation and development programmes.

Aslib Proceedings
London: Aslib, The Association for Information management.
12 issues a year (ISSN 0001 253X).

Contains published papers from Aslib meetings and conferences, together with articles on new products and equipment, and practical techniques and systems in information management.

Electronic and Optical Publishing Review
Oxford: Learned Information (Europe) Ltd.
4 issues a year (ISSN 0951 7154).

An international journal devoted to coverage of the transfer of published information through digital electronic media (videotex, online and CD-ROM).

Government Information Quarterly
Greenwich, CT: JAI Press, Inc.
4 issues a year (ISSN 0740 624X).

A cross-disciplinary journal offering a forum for theoretical and philosophical analysis of government information activities. Discusses current policies and practices in the provision of services and the management of resources, aimed at government officials, policy makers and those interested in the role of government information in society.

Government Publications Review
Oxford: Pergamon Press plc.
6 issues a year (ISSN 0277 9390).

A US journal covering all aspects of government publications handling, availability and selection, and Federal information resource management and dissemination.

Information Age
Guildford: Butterworth Scientific Ltd.
4 issues a year (ISSN 0261 4103),

Covers policy, economics, law and information and their societal impact.

Information Economics and Policy
Amsterdam: Elsevier Science Publishers BV (North-Holland).
4 issues a year (ISSN 0167 6245).

A largely theoretical journal covering the relationships between telecommunications, information economics and media/information policy.

The Information Society
London: Taylor & Francis Ltd.
4 issues a year (ISSN 0197 2243).

Provides a forum for the discussion of significant topics in the information sector. These include: transborder data flow; regulatory issues; the impact of the information industries on society; and information as a determinant of public and private organisational performance.

Information Technology and Public Policy
London: Parliamentary Information Technology Committee (PITCOM).
3 issues a year (ISSN 0266 851399).

The journal and Proceedings of the Parliamentary Information Technology Committee. Includes articles on all areas relating to computer software and hardware matters, from a wide range of perspectives from industry to academia. Also includes coverage of parliamentary activity: written and oral questions and answers and transcripts of debates.

InterMedia
London: International Institute of Communications (IIC).
6 issues a year (ISSN 0309 118X).

Journal covering the full range of issues surrounding the communication of information and ideas. Coverage includes new communication technologies; broadcasting and telecommunications; media and communications policy; copyright and data protection; and the social and cultural impacts of the information industries.

International Journal of Information and Library Research
London: Taylor Graham Publishing.
3 issues a year (ISSN 0953 556X).

Current research and development in information management and information technology, incorporating both qualitative and quantitative approaches to research directed at library and information managers, publishers and communication specialists and students of information science and librarianship.

Journal of Information Science
Amsterdam: Elsevier Science Publishers BV (North-Holland).
6 issues a year (ISSN 0165 5515).

Reports developments and theories in mechanised information systems, covering: office automation; communications; technology transfer and innovation; writing, publishing and transmission; and information management.

Library Association Record
London: Library Association Publishing Ltd.
12 issues a year (ISSN 0024 2195).

Contains articles and news relevant to those working in librarianship and information science.

Library & Information Briefings
London: Library & Information Technology Centre, on behalf of the British Library
8 issues a year (ISSN 0954 1829).

A series of management briefs covering key aspects of library and information science. Recent issues have included: Open Systems Interconnection (1); CD-ROM (3); Public/private sector relationships (5); and Integrated Services Digital Networks (8).

Library and Information Research News
London: Library and Information Research Group.
4 issues a year (ISSN 0141 6561).

Articles, news and reviews relating to library and information research and its application in practice. Includes research papers, project reports, reports of seminars and conferences, and editorial comment.

Online Review
Oxford: Learned Information Ltd.
6 issues a year (ISSN 0309 314X).

Journal covering the whole field of online information. Contains articles from both academics and practitioners on areas including the major online services, databases and communications networks; data protection; transborder data flows; copyright; as well as more practical articles relating to searching specific databases.

Policy Studies
London: Policy Studies Institute (PSI).
4 issues a year (ISSN 0144 2872).

Critical journal of the Policy Studies Institute, containing articles on economic, industrial and social policy and the workings of political institutions.

Telecommunications Policy
London: Butterworth & Co. (Publishing) Ltd
6 issues a year (ISSN 0308 5961).

Covers the regulation and management of telecommunications and information systems.

Telematics and Informatics
Oxford: Pergamon Press plc.
3 issues a year (ISSN 0736 5853).

An international journal containing information on applied telecommunications and information technology; information resources management; the socio-economic implications of information; information policy and legislation; and international issues in communication.

Transnational Data and Communications Report
Washington, DC: Transnational Data Reporting Service.
10 issues a year (ISSN 0892 399X).

An international journal focussing on trade in data services, data protection and copyright legislation. Includes much useful information about the activities of national and international organisations like the Council of Europe and the United Nations.

ABSTRACTING & INDEXING SERVICES

CABLIS (Current Awareness Bulletin for Library and Information Staff)
London: British Library Research and Development Department (ceased publication December 1990)
12 issues a year (ISSN 0954 9196).

Abstracts relevant journal articles in the field of library and information services, as well as carrying its own news regarding the activities of the British Library and acquisitions information for the BLISS information service.

Electronic Publishing Abstracts
Oxford: Pergamon Press plc, on behalf of Pira.
12 issues a year (ISSN 0739 2907), also available as an online file (EPUBS) on ORBIT Search Service.

Provides summaries of scientific and technical literature in electronic publishing and information technology. In particular, it covers the transmission, storage and retrieval of text and images as an alternative to the publication of printed documents.

Library and Information Science Abstracts (LISA)
London: Library Association Publishing Ltd.
12 issues a year (ISSN 0024 2179), also available as an online file on DIALOG Information Services (file 61) or ORBIT Search Service; and as a CD-ROM service by subscription from SilverPlatter Information Inc.

Monthly abstracting covering the major journals in information science, publishing and librarianship.

Science and TechnologyPolicy
London: The British Library Board.
6 issues a year (ISSN 0952 9616).

A review of current national press comment, scientific reports and other documentary material covering areas such as the state of British science; industrial competitiveness; employment, training and skills shortages; research and development activity; and regional and sectoral trends.

6. List of acronyms and abbreviations

ACARD	Advisory Council for Applied Research and Development
ACSP	Advisory Council on Scientific Policy
ACSTI	Advisory Committee for Scientific and Technical Information
AGI	Association for Geographic Information
Aslib	Association for Information Management
BBC	British Broadcasting Corporation
BL	British Library
BLAISE	British Library Automated Information Service
BLBSD	British Library Bibliographic Services Division
BLDSC	British Library Document Supply Centre (formerly British Library Lending Division)
BLEND	Birmingham and Loughborough Electronic Network Development
BLLD	British Library Lending Division
BLRD&D	British Library Research & Development Department
BNB	British National Bibliography
BT	British Telecom
CAB	Commonwealth Agricultural Bureaux
CADAPSO	Information Industries Committee (Canada)
CBAC	Chemical and Biological Activities (Chemical Abstracts)
CBURC	Computer Board for Universities and Research Councils
CEC	Commission of the European Communities
CCIS	Centre for Communication and Information Studies, Polytechnic of Central London
CICI	Confederation of Information Communication Industries
CIDST	Committee for Information and Documentation in Science and Technology
CoE	Council of Europe

DES	Department of Education and Science
DIANE	Direct Access Network for Europe
DoI	Department of Industry
DPA	Data Protection Authority
DPC	Document Processing Centre
DSIR	Department for Scientific and Industrial Research
DTI	Department of Trade and Industry
EDI	electronic data interchange
EHOG	European Host Operators Group
EIIA	European Information Industries Association
EIS	electronic information services
ESA	European Space Agency
ESRC	Economic and Social Research Council
Eusidic	European Association of Information Services (formerly European Scientific Information Dissemination Centres)
FID	International Federation for Information and Documentation
GAIIA	Global Alliance of Information Industry Associations
GAIT	General Agreement on Information Trade
GATT	General Agreement on Tariffs and Trade
GFFIL	French Association of Online Information Providers
HMSO	Her Majesty's Stationery Office
IBA	Independent Broadcasting Authority
IBM	International Business Machines
ICCSTI	Interdepartmental Co-ordinating Committee for Scientific and Technical Information
ICTs	information and communication technologies
IDST	Information and Documentation in Science and Technology
IFLA	International Federation of Library Associations
IIA	Information Industries Association (US)
IIC	International Institute of Communications
IIS	Institute of Information Scientists
ILO	Industrial Liaison Scheme
IMPACT	Information Market Policy Actions
Inspec	Information Service for the Physics and Engineering Communities
IRPP	Institute for Research on Public Policy
ISIC	International Standard Industrial Classification
ISO	International Standards Organisation

IT	information technology
ITAP	Information Technology Advisory Panel
ITUSA	Information Technology Users Standards Association
JANET	Joint Academic Network
JCC	Joint Consultative Committee
LA	Library Association
LAC-E	Library Advisory Council for England
LAC-W	Library Advisory Council for Wales
LINC	Loughborough Information Network Community
LIP	Library and Information Plan
LISA	Library and Information Science Abstracts
LISC	Library and Information Services Council
MARC	Machine-Readable Cataloguing
MAP	Microprocessor Applications Project
MEDLARS	Medical Literature Analysis and Retrieval System
MinTech	Ministry of Technology
NAB	National Advisory Board for Public Sector Higher Education
NCCL	National Council for Civil Liberties
NCL	National Central Library
NCLIS	National Commission on Libraries and Information Science (US)
NLLST	National Lending Library for Science and Technology
NOBIN	Nederlandse Irgaan voor de Bevordering van de Informatieverezorging (Netherlands)
NRLSI	National Reference Library for Science and Invention
NTIS	National Technical Information Service (US)
OAL	Office of Arts and Libraries
OECD	Organisation for Economic Co-operation and Development
OSTI	Office for Scientific and Technical Information
OTA	Office of Technology Assessment (US)
PICT	Programme on Information and Communication Technologies
PITCOM	Parliamentary Information Technology Committee
POLIS	Parliamentary Online Information System
PSI	Policy Studies Institute

SCONUL	Standing Conference on National and University Libraries
SDC	System Development Corporation
SPRU	Science Policy Research Unit, University of Sussex
STM	science, technology and medicine
TBDF	transborder data flows
TMA	Telecommunications Managers Association
UGC	University Grants Committee
UKCIS	United Kingdom Chemical Information Service
UNESCO	United Nations Education, Scientific and Cultural Organisation
VADS	Value Added and Data Services
VANS	Value Added Network Services